STAGE MANAGEMENT

STAGE MANAGEMENT

THE ESSENTIAL HANDBOOK

Gail Pallin

QUEENSGATE PUBLICATIONS

First published in 2000 by Queensgate Publications, Cookham, Berkshire

© Queensgate Securities Ltd, 2000
Text © Gail Pallin, 2000

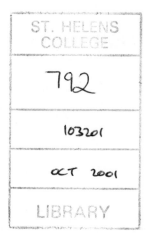
Photography by Colin Cavers
Illustrations by Mark Richards
Cover design by Charlie Webster
Book design by Production Line, Minster Lovell, Oxford
Production by Landmark Consultants, Princes Risborough, Buckinghamshire
Printed in Finland by WSOY

ISBN 1-902655-08-7

A catalogue record of this book is available from the British Library.

DEDICATION

This book is dedicated to all Queen Margaret University College students and fellow professionals – past and present – who have challenged and inspired me. I have no doubt that they will continue to do so in the future!

ABOUT THE AUTHOR

Gail Pallin is Subject Leader in Stage Management at Queen Margaret University College, Edinburgh. Educated and trained in Scotland, she began her career in Stage Management at the Royal Lyceum Theatre, Edinburgh. Since then she has worked at many of the major Repertory theatres in Britain, including Pitlochry Festival Theatre and the Haymarket Theatre, Leicester. One of her most challenging and exciting posts was as Stage Manager on the original production of ROAD, by Jim Cartwright, at The Royal Court Theatre in London.

ACKNOWLEDGEMENTS

Particular thanks are due to Colin Cavers, Mark Richards, Kevin Eld and Alan Ayckbourn for their invaluable contributions to the text.

And thanks also to those whose support and advice meant not only that the manuscript was delivered on time, but also that it was delivered at all! They are, in no particular order, Greta Millington, Mike Griffiths, Gary Sparkes, Lorne Boswell, Peter Byard, Madeleine Campbell, John Stone, Roy McMahon, Alison Steele, Roland Chadwick, Paul Rummer, Julian Bryant, Jimmy and Florie Pallin, Nigel Jones, Corrie Cooper, Andrew Usher, Tracy Cattell, Derek McGhie, Joclynn Roberts, Victoria Fleming, Natasha Lee Walsh, Tracey Robertson, Gareth Pritchard, Lee Malcolmson, John Ramage, Lynn Bains, Pauline Miller Judd, Ronnie Smith, Ben Tinniswood, Scott Anderson, Molly Johnson, Jan Bee Brown, Peter Donald, John Diamond, Emma Whitfield, Ross McDade and Gemma Smith.

CONTENTS

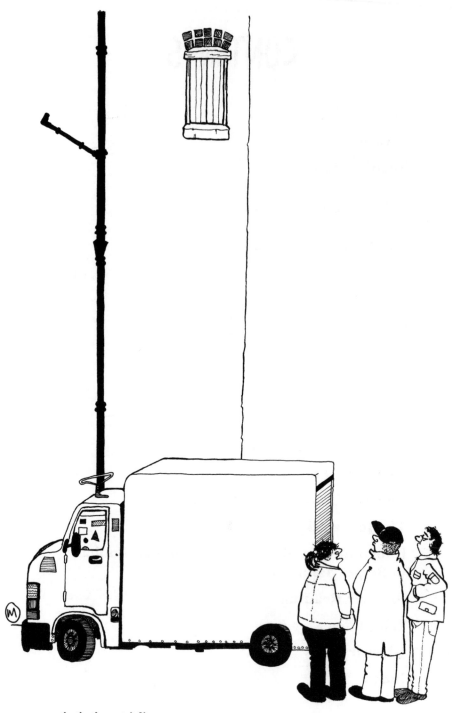

'What do you mean, that's the get-in?'

FOREWORD

Over thirty years ago I sneaked into professional theatre via the then established back door employed by the untrained aspiring actor or director who, for one reason or another, had chosen to eschew the formal entry route through drama school. I became an acting Assistant Stage Manager (ASM). Underpaid, if paid at all, this underclass was trapped between full time career Stage Manager and the fully-fledged actor. Stage Managers regarded acting ASMs with a mixture of amusement and contempt. Acting ASMs, in their professional experience, sat for hours in prop rooms taking three days doing a task badly that would have taken them three minutes to do well, dreaming of the day when they too would tread the boards. Acting ASMs, during performances, often performed their stage managerial duties while still wearing their stage costumes. I once worked the fly gallery in a rather skimpy sarong. I'd never climbed a ladder quite so fast.

Actors (the proper ones) tolerated us, albeit with a certain wariness. We were, after all, inaudible, untrained amateurs wearing rather too much stage make-up and often having a tenuous grasp of the text. We were an economic liability foist upon them by a penny-pinching management. We were doing the job that should properly have been done by a trained actor.

In the social order of things acting ASMs could be classed as the tweenies of the theatre. There was, in those days, still a residue of the old theatrical class system left over from a pre-war era which decreed that, while actors were above stairs, stage management belonged very much below stairs. Rarely did the two mix socially. In 1967, when my first West End play was doing its pre-London tour, Celia Johnson invited the company, cast and stage management to Sunday lunch at her home near Oxford. Celia was adored by us all as much for her charming self as for her formidable talent. Nonetheless there was a certain social embarrassment when, lunch having been announced, Celia indicated that the sole stage management representative among her guests would be eating separately from the rest of the party in the kitchen with nanny. So fondly was Celia regarded that no one present had the heart to say anything.

In the space of my lifetime I have seen and, needless to say, applauded the change in attitude between the two. Rightly and properly, the relationship between stage manager and performer has become a closer one with (in general!) each respecting the other's craft. I did once have to stop a stage manager, driven to his hysterical limit by an offstage cast devouring his carefully prepared sandwiches, from spraying the food with a mild poison.

Part of this new found respectability is undoubtedly due to the demise of the acting ASM. Stage Management is no longer regarded as something that any passing body can take up at a moment's notice. Part, too, is the seriousness now given to training. With the growth of backstage technology, the running of even a quite straightforward show these days requires enormous presence of mind, cool nerve and fast reflexes.

As a director of a small regional company, I spend most of my year in rehearsal. Other than the cast, the only permanent observer of the production's progress is the Deputy Stage Manager (DSM). She or he (usually she) is our only day to day link with the rest of the building, passing on decisions, potential problems and possible conflicts of interest between departments ('Design department: Miss Jones is now climbing out on to the roof in her crinoline, can both windows be made to open fully, please.'). Importantly for the director, the DSM becomes another pair of eyes. How often have I sneaked a covert glance towards my companion to see if the faint smile still approves the comic climax, or that the blink rate has gone up ever so slightly at the tragic denouement.

I'm delighted to have been asked to write the Foreword to this valuable book. It's long overdue: a comprehensive guide for the aspiring stage manager, full of possible gentle reminders for the more experienced practitioner and for the curious layman a positive eye opener.

ALAN AYCKBOURN
Scarborough, September 1999

INTRODUCTION

by Kevin Eld

This is a book written by a stage manager for stage managers. It is aimed at students of stage management and theatre arts, newly qualified professionals, amateurs, arts centres, community drama workers, event organisers and anyone with an interest in learning more about an extremely challenging and rewarding show business discipline.

When one knows a great deal about a subject, and has practised a profession for many years, the questions 'How do I begin?' or 'Where shall I start?' always exist, but they are dealt with in the subconscious – much like pressing the accelerator and releasing the clutch when pulling away in a car. Consequently, to answer them correctly can be a more difficult and challenging task than was first thought.

I started in theatre as a stagehand at the tender age of 16. I worked for many years in a large, modern repertory theatre in the Midlands, where I was lucky enough to experience everything from touring opera to contemporary dance and from *Equus* to *My Fair Lady*. I toured the world with *Hamlet* and worked on a production of Shakespeare's *Julius Caesar* which played every major city in India. After moving to the West End I worked with Sir Cameron Mackintosh for several years and production managed many large musicals for him including the UK's first touring production of *The Phantom of the Opera*, which travelled in more than 35 40ft trailers. In every case the show was held together by the stage manager.

After 25 years in the business I feel qualified to say that whether the show is a multi-million pound West End musical or a local amateur production, the same basic rules apply. The stage manager is the 'hub of the wheel' for the production team and company alike, and must know the text and blocking of a piece equally as well as the director. The show is unlikely to run smoothly or be a success if it is poorly stage-managed.

Gail Pallin and I first met in the late 1980s, when I was the production manager in the main house and she was the production manager of the studio theatre, and occasionally deputy on main house shows. She has dedicated her professional life to the art of the stage manager and there can be no one better qualified to write this book. We share many happy memories of our partnership and were a great team. We argued together and fought as all good partners do from time to time, but most of all we laughed and had fun.

I recall one particular episode, we were working on a production of the musical *High Society*. The set was somewhat ill conceived and involved many trucks arriving onstage by means of tracks that crossed each other in the wings. In fact one of the stage management team was heard to comment 'being backstage on this show is more akin to working for British Rail than British rep'. One of the said trucks was a full size swimming pool and on the night in question the pool became jammed between two tracks. It would go neither on nor off stage, and was unfortunately wedged in position in full view of a packed auditorium. We decided that the only thing to do was to place several burly stage crew on the offstage end of the stubborn truck and on the command everyone would give a big heave. If only life were that simple. Instead of the pool moving smoothly off stage in the semi blackout, the entire end tore away accompanied by the very loud sound of ripping plywood. The lights came up to reveal the stagehands lying on their backs with their legs in the air! Gail still insists that no one noticed, but I'm not so sure.

There are many different types of theatre in existence, and as many varieties of stage managers. The job role will depend on the scale of the show, and the size of the staffing budgets. The basic principles in this book relate to stage management techniques used in middle scale repertory theatre. Although not as commonplace today as it was, repertory theatre still thrives in the UK and many companies still perform different pieces on alternate nights. Indeed this is still the way many opera and dance companies prefer to operate.

Small scale touring continues to be a wonderful training ground for the novice assistant stage manager, where one can learn the trade from seasoned professionals and develop the skills that have changed little since the days of William Shakespeare. The next logical step might be to investigate the world of commercial touring, ballet, opera or musical theatre, where the budgets are larger and the sets, special effects, lighting and sound rigs are generally more complex. This is where one starts to come into contact with the cutting edge of theatre technology as well as higher profile performers and creative teams.

You may have the opportunity to work on a long running production in the West End where you will meet new challenges, such as maintaining the motivation of the team and company, as well as the look of the show, after many months or, in some cases, years of doing the same show every night. This is the place where you may well encounter the black art of the automated set, where huge pieces of scenery are controlled with pinpoint accuracy by what appears to be a tiny computer. Complex scene changes can be plotted where several flown pieces pass each other while trucks negotiate their way across a revolving stage, and all under the control of one individual!

Whichever area you find yourself in, one thing is certain: you will become nurse maid, confidant and agony aunt to many different and unlikely people. Life will never be dull and you will experience tremendous highs and bottomless lows. The experience of saying 'Stand-by LX cue 1' and 'House tabs – Go' will give you a rush of adrenaline that few other experiences in life can.

Kevin Eld is Vice President of Production and Creative Entertainment for EuroDisney

CHAPTER 1

TEAM DYNAMICS AND ROLES

In any group the key to productivity is teamwork. This alludes to the need for an integrated, co-operative and symbiotic relationship between all members. Central to this is the ability of each individual to be adaptable. This will lead to a sense of camaraderie and successful outcomes to team goals. It is essential to realise that a good team will share their skills, abilities and experience in an interactive and flexible way. The diagram below shows the relationship between the various roles within a producing theatre company.

Please note this is just one model of many, and each company will vary depending on its size, financial status and artistic scope. The diagram is somewhat hierarchical, but is useful to demonstrate the layers of responsibility and practical connections between the directors, front of house and producing departments. A more symbiotic diagram is shown at the end of this chapter.

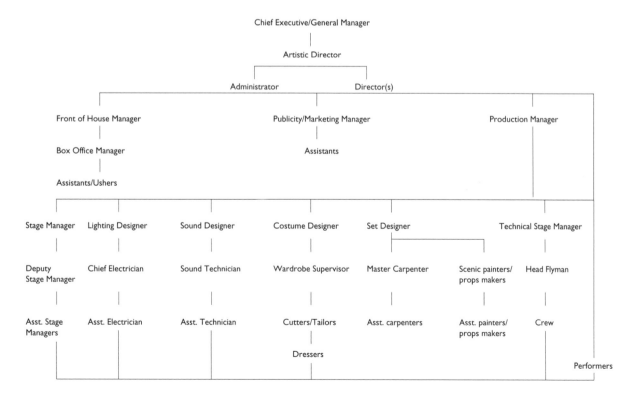

Job roles

As with the diagram above, the responsibilities of the team will differ from company to company. The following descriptions are based loosely on middle to large scale repertory theatre, but can be applied to most companies.

General Manager

- Reports directly to the board of governors.
- Has overall responsibility for the general running of the theatre.
- Liases with the board and artistic director on strategic planning and artistic policies.
- Works with the artistic director and the board to ensure building and staffing costs stay within the yearly budgets allocated.
- Oversees and staffs the front of house and marketing departments.
- In liaison with the board of directors, negotiates contractual terms and engages the artistic director.

Artistic Director

- Liases with the general manager on the artistic remit, strategic planning and monetary allocations of the company.
- Hires directors and designers.
- Plans the season with respect to in-house and visiting productions.
- Directs a few productions out of the season.
- Liases with marketing and publicity in developing sponsorship and marketing policies.

Director

- Has overall artistic control of the production they have been hired to direct.
- Liases with the designers to create the style and concepts integral to the production.
- Responsible for directing the performers, and advising all production departments as to the requirements of the production.
- Maintains an overview of the piece to ensure a cohesive production.
- Liases with the production manager to ensure budgetary control.

Administrator

- Controls, administrates and keeps account of all spending within the company.
- Responsible for employees' rights and pay.
- Originates and distributes allocated budgets to the managers.

Production Manager (PM)

- Employs and supervises all production staff.
- Plans and maintains staffing levels.
- Ensures the staff is trained in safe working practices as required by the Health and Safety policy.

- Responsible for the maintenance and safety of all working areas and equipment as required by the Health and Safety policy.
- Liaises and agrees the budgets and design deadlines with the director and designers.
- Advises the designer about health and safety implications within the set design.
- Prepares and distributes the provisional schedule and budgets to all production departments.
- Oversees all ordering of materials and building work.
- Manages and controls the production budget.
- Chairs design and production/ progress meetings.
- Prepares the production risk assessment and advises on action to be taken.
- Schedules and oversees all work during production week.
- Contributes to the technical rehearsal by taking technical notes and scheduling their completion.
- Attends the first performance to confirm the director's original intent has been achieved.

Stage Manager (SM)

- Has overall responsibility for the stage management team and their training, but should be prepared to do any and all work within the team's remit.
- Oversees auditions, and provides and furnishes rehearsal space with a mark up, rehearsal props, furniture and elements of the set at the director's discretion.
- Co-ordinates the information flow between all departments.
- Oversees the rehearsal process, company calls and overtime payments pertaining to union agreements.
- Ensures rehearsals comply with the Health and Safety policy.
- Organises and participates in the research, procurement and safe storage of props, furniture and set dressing, and their safe return.
- Manages the stage management budget.
- Runs the technical rehearsal in liaison with the director, production manager and deputy stage manager.
- Responsible for the health and well-being of the company, and all aspects of the show during the run (including maintaining the quality of performance).
- Organises and manages the safe return of props and furniture.

Deputy Stage Manager (DSM)

- Assists with auditions and preparation of rehearsal room.
- Compiles provisional props list in conjunction with the stage manager and assistant stage manager.
- Sets up and runs rehearsals daily.
- Responsible for blocking, prompting and distributing rehearsal notes and call sheets daily.
- Keeps record of performers' hours with respect to union agreement.
- Compiles and distributes setting plots, running plots and cue synopsis.
- Advises stage manager of any health and safety issues within rehearsals.
- Cues show during the technical rehearsal, dresses and the run.

- Writes up the show report after every performance to assist in maintaining discipline and quality of performance and technical standards throughout the run.
- Ensures all running plots are appended to the prompt copy at the end of the run.
- Assists with the safe return of props and furniture.
- May be required to deputise for the stage manager.

Assistant Stage Manager (ASM)

- Assists with auditions and preparation of rehearsal room.
- Participates in the procurement of props, furniture and set dressing.
- Covers rehearsals if necessary.
- Works within the allocated stage management budget.
- Has a major responsibility for the setting of props and backstage work during the run, which frees up the stage manager to troubleshoot.
- Assists with the safe return of props and furniture.
- May be required to deputise for the deputy stage manager.

Set Designer

- Liases with the director to conceive the visual and stylistic elements of the set, furniture and props.
- Builds a scale model of the set, and produces a ground plan and working drawings to assist the production team and performers to visualise the ideas contained in the design.
- Works with the director, costume and lighting designer to ensure a visual cohesion throughout the design.
- In liaison with the production manager, ensures the design is within budget and every effort has been taken to provide a safe environment for the performers to work within.
- Oversees the building, painting, fit up and technical and dress rehearsals to ensure the original intentions are realised.

Master Carpenter

- Responsible for building the set within the time allocated.
- Trains and oversees all work done by the assistants.
- Ensures all work done by workshop staff comply with Health and Safety regulations.
- Controls the budget allocated for the build.
- May run the fit up and is responsible for the safe delivery of the set onstage.
- Ensures the quality of the set is maintained throughout the run.

Scenic Painter

- Oversees the smooth running of the paint shop.
- Responsible for painting all elements of the set within the time allocated.
- Ensures assistants are adequately trained and observe the Health and Safety legislation in their use of the many and various materials required for the job.
- Controls the paint budget.

Props Master

• Oversees the smooth running of the prop shop.
• Is responsible for delivering all props makes within the time allocated.
• Ensures assistants are adequately trained and observe the Health and Safety legislation in their handling of dangerous substances and equipment.
• Controls the props makes budget.
• Assists stage management in maintaining a high standard of props throughout the run.

'Complaining about the chief chippy's build techniques during a fit up shows a lack of tact and probably doesn't help team dynamics.'

Lighting Designer

• In liaison with the director and set and costume designers, develops the overall lighting interpretation for the production within the allocated budget.
• Decides on the most appropriate types of lamps, effects and other specialist equipment required to achieve the design.
• Chooses the most appropriate positions for lighting and auxiliary equipment and produces a plan to convey that design for rigging.

- Ensures the consistent quality of the three dimensional lighting picture.
- Trains (if necessary) the lighting technician who is operating the show, and oversees the plotting session, technical rehearsal, dresses and first night to ensure the design is true to the original intent.

Chief LX (electrician)

- Manages the smooth running of the electrical department.
- Responsible for maintaining all in-house electrical equipment with respect to Health and Safety legislation.
- Responsible for rigging, focusing and plotting in the allocated time.
- Trains and oversees all work done by the assistants.
- Sources hires and effects and controls the departmental budget.
- Ensures the quality of the lighting design is maintained throughout the run.

Sound Designer

- In liaison with the director and musical director (where relevant), designs the overall sound for the production within the allocated budget.
- In consultation with the production manager, will choose the most appropriate types and positions for speakers, monitors, mixers and auxiliary equipment.
- Ensures the quality of sound from the front row of the audience right up to the gods is balanced and audible.
- Trains the sound technician operating the show, and oversees the technical rehearsal, dresses and first night to ensure the design is true to the original intent.

Sound Technician

- Responsible for ensuring all in-house sound equipment is maintained to a high standard.
- Hires and orders equipment needed for the show.
- Records sound effects required for the production.
- Operates the sound during the run, and maintains the standards of sound quality, as designed, throughout the run.

Costume Designer

- In liaison with the director and set and lighting designers, will conceive the visual and stylistic designs of the costumes.
- Provides costume plates/drawings and fabric samples for the wardrobe supervisor to realise the designs.
- In consultation with the production manager and wardrobe supervisor, ensures the expenditure comes within the budget.
- Oversees the making and hiring of costumes and attends all fittings.
- Attends technical dress rehearsals and the first night to ensure the original intentions have been achieved.

Wardrobe Supervisor

- Manages the smooth running of the wardrobe.
- Responsible for the delivery of all costumes within the time allocated.
- Trains the wardrobe staff and oversees making and hiring of costumes.
- Ensures all work done in wardrobe complies with the health and safety policy.
- Orders all materials necessary for the costume makes.
- Controls the costume budget.
- Runs the fittings and costume parade/call to ensure the performers are comfortable and happy with their costumes.
- Attends the technical, dress rehearsals and first night to ensure the original intention has been realised.

Cutters/Tailors

- Works to the designs provided by the costume designer.
- Builds all costumes within the time allocated.
- Observes safe working practices within wardrobe.
- Attends the technical, dress rehearsals and first night to take notes of required alterations.

Dressers/maintenance

- Responsible for the costume changes during the technical, dress rehearsals and the run.
- Ensures the performers are assisted with any difficulties they may have pertaining to the costumes or costume changes.
- Maintains the costumes throughout the run to provide a constant quality of appearance.

Technical Stage Manager

- Responsible for all moving elements of the set.
- In liaison with the production manager, lighting designer and flyman allocates each piece of flown scenery to a specific bar.
- Manages the crew, and plans the scene changes.
- Oversees and trains staff where necessary in respect of technical work onstage.
- Ensures the moving elements of the set comply with Health and Safety regulations, and staff are trained and equipped correctly.
- Oversees all technical onstage work during production week and the run.

Head Flyman

- Maintains the fly floor and flying system.
- Responsible for the safe rigging of all flown pieces of scenery complying with Health and Safety regulations.
- Trains other crew working on the fly floor.
- Compiles the flying plot and operates the show.

Crew

- Mainly employed on a show-by-show basis to supplement permanent staff.
- Assist with get ins, fit ups, scene changes, flying, follow spotting, get outs etc.
- Complies with all Health and Safety regulations as stipulated by the production manager.

Front of House/Box Office Manager

- Responsible for the auditorium, restaurant and bar areas and box office.
- Ensures the health and well-being of the audience in respect of the health and safety policy.
- Manages and trains bar and restaurant staff, ushers and support staff.
- In liaison with the publicity manager, hangs the front of house displays.

Marketing/Publicity Manager

- Responsible for selling the show, and raising the public profile of the theatre.
- In liaison with the general manager and artistic director attracts sponsorship in order to raise funds and revenue.
- Produces posters, leaflets and advertising and organises their distribution. Arranges press and photo calls with the performers in liaison with the stage manager.

Things they never said

Extract from 'Flyman' *(The Stage and Television Today)*

ASM	The Director liked all the props we got today.
PM	Ah ha, a revolve. Terrific.
Chippie	I don't know, let's look at the ground plan.
Set Designer	Well, let's just have whatever is cheaper.
Sound	Better turn that down a bit. We don't want to deafen them.
Director	Sorry, my mistake.
Electrics	This equipment is more complicated than we need.
Performer	I really think my big scene should be cut.

The wheel of communication

One of the many functions of the stage management team is to ensure the effective flow of communication to and from all departments.

One type of communication network is shown opposite. The stage management team is the hub of a wheel with other production departments relying on information feeding in and out of the team accurately and efficiently. The production manager is a satellite encompassing all departments.

The following key is a guide to the abbreviations below and throughout this book.

SMgt	Stage Management	PM	Production Manager
SM	Stage Manager	DSM	Deputy Stage Manager
ASM	Assistant Stage Manager	LX	Lighting (department)
Reh	Rehearsals	FoH	Front of House.

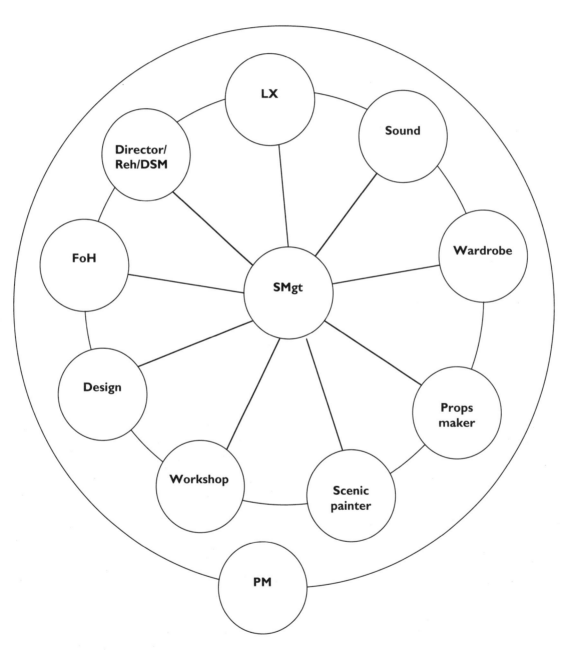

CHAPTER 2
THE PREPARATION PERIOD

Having decided which play your company wishes to produce there are many tasks to consider and achieve. The following activities have to be accomplished before rehearsals can begin:

1. Performing rights
2. Provisional schedule
3. Budget allocations
4. Book rehearsal space
5. Auditions
6. Textual analysis / design
7. Prepare rehearsal room
8. Prepare prompt copy
9. First day of rehearsals

Performing rights

Once the director has decided which play they wish to produce it is necessary to write to the playwright or agent to gain permission to put the play on in front of a paying audience. If permission is granted a fee will be paid. Usually a payment is not required if the playwright has been dead for 70 years. When in doubt consult the publisher. The responsibility for this will depend on the type of company it is. This process can take quite a lot of time and effort so if you are starting from scratch, plan ahead, and gain permission before contracting production staff or performers! At this point one can order scripts and ensure all the designers and production team get copies.

Provisional schedule

The production manager will create a provisional schedule, which details the order of events. This enables all departments to keep within the time constraints of any given production. The schedule begins with the initial design meetings and will end around the opening night. It should include the following key features:

- Design deadlines for set, costume, LX, sound and FoH
- Design meetings

- Production/progress meetings
- Rough outline of the production week.
- Props call/spread
- Costume call/parade

All heads of department will be consulted during this process and once agreement has been reached the production manager will distribute a copy to all relevant production team members, designers and director. A more detailed production schedule is drawn up by the production manager later on during the build period. Please note that this schedule is not issued to performers. The director, in collaboration with the deputy stage manager (DSM) provides the performers with a rehearsal schedule on a daily or weekly basis.

Example of a provisional schedule:

1 March		Initial design meeting
10 March		Design meeting
17 March		Set and costume designs finalised
22 March	AM	Read through. Set & costume presentation
	PM	Props meeting
23 March	AM	Rehearsals and build begins
26 March	AM	Production meeting
2 April	AM	Production meeting
7 April	PM	Credit deadline
		Props deadline
8 April	PM	Props call
		Costume call
9 April	AM	Production meeting
	PM	LX and sound deadline
10 April	AM	Final run through
	Eve	Strike/Rigg
11 April		Fit up
12 April		Focus
13 April		Plot
14 April		Technical
15 April		Tech/Dress
16 April		Dress/Preview

Budget allocations

The production manager will either be issued or will negotiate the production budget with the director/general manager/administrator. This grand total should be sufficient to cover all the production costs and sometimes may have to include overtime and casual labour (crew working the fit up and show, extra assistants in wardrobe, additional carpenters, upholsterers, props makers etc.)

In consultation with all the heads of departments, the PM will work out how much each department needs to realise the design, then allocate a realistic figure, ensuring the total stays within the grand total. The amount the stage management (SMgt) team is allocated depends entirely on the type and style of production and what the team is responsible for acquiring.

Here are examples of the variety of SMgt budgets one might come across:

- Small scale/Small scale touring   £50–150
- Middle scale rep   £80–1000
- Large scale rep/Touring   £500–2000
- London theatres/West end   £1000–3000

Book rehearsal space

The stage manager (SM) should think carefully about the requirements of the company and production when booking a rehearsal space, unless you are fortunate enough to have a rehearsal room or two on site. Some elements to be considered:

- Adequate size
- Heating and floor surface (especially important if there are dancers)
- Lighting (natural if possible)
- Toilet/shower facilities
- Changing room/green room
- Ventilation
- Privacy/noise insulation
- Kitchen facilities
- Location (parking, easy access by local transport etc)

Auditions

The SMgt team assist with auditions where possible to help the process run smoothly and to collate a running order with timings for each performer being auditioned. It is useful to have the DSM in the audition room assisting the director and another member of the team outside the room making sure each person is standing by for their turn.

Textual analysis/design

The designer meets with the director to discuss the style, period and look of the production. After much discussion they will agree on a design. Having read the script and conducted extensive research, the SMgt team, in consultation with the designer, can then prepare a list of all the props, furniture and set dressing. The designer will prepare a model, working drawings and a ground plan. The latter will be given to the SMgt team to realise the mark up.

The model

The model is an accurate 3-D representation of the set using the scale of 1:25. It affords the director, performers and production team a detailed visual representation to work from during rehearsals and the build period. The carpenters, scenic painters and SMgt team will refer to it constantly for information on colour, shape and size of all the elements of the scenery and furniture. For example, if the SMgt team are unsure of the colour of the cushions, vase, sofa etc, then they can refer to the model then try to match the colour shown there.

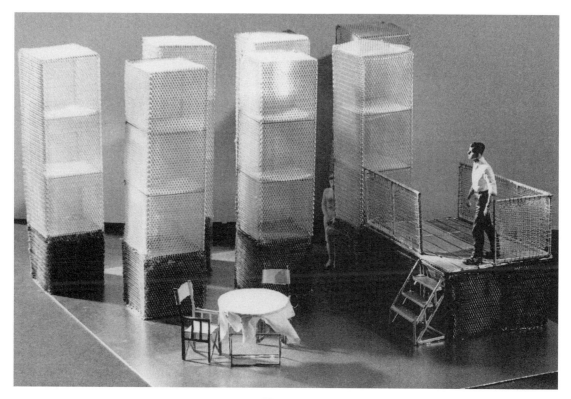

The model

The ground plan

The ground plan is an accurate scaled 2-D representation of the set as seen from above – a bird's eye view. It will also give additional information about the layout of the stage area *(see page 34)*.

Ground plan symbols Most designers use the same basic symbols to represent flats, trucks, windows, furniture etc. Here are some examples:

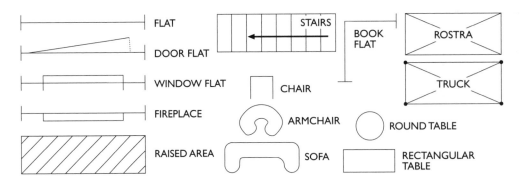

In order to read the ground plan, and translate the measurements for the mark up, the team will need to feel comfortable using a scale rule. Most British companies work in the scale of 1:25.

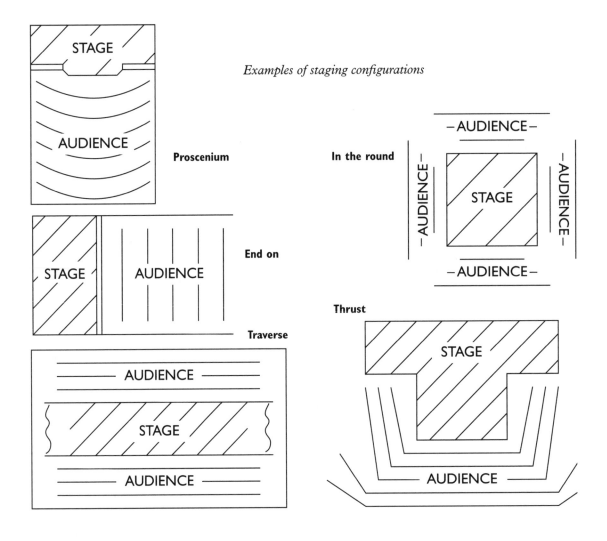

Examples of staging configurations

Prepare the rehearsal room

Ensure your space is clean and tidy. It may be necessary to sweep and mop the floor which will help the LX tape to stay put!

Mark-up

Marking up consists of translating the design from the ground plan on to the floor of the rehearsal room. The mark-up kit should consist of the following items:

- 2 x tape measures (1x10m, 1x20m)
- Scale rule (1:25)
- LX tape
- Scissors/stanley knife
- Pencil
- Chalk line
- Chalk
- String (for circles)

There are two basic methods. The first is quicker but not as accurate, the second comes highly recommended.

The 90 degree method:

On ground plan	**On floor**
Decide on setting line	Mark setting line with chalk line then LX tape
Measure centre line from A – B	Translate measurement to floor and mark B
Measure 90 degrees from B – C	Translate measurement to find C

Ground plan showing flatage for box-set (not to scale):

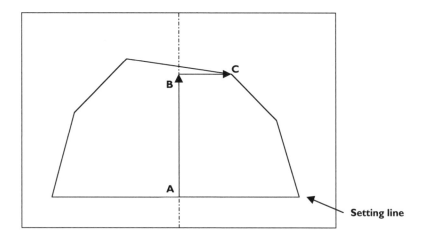

The triangulation method:

This requires a minimum of two people, three if possible. One person on tape A, one on tape B, and one reading off measurements from the ground plan.

On ground plan	**On floor**
Decide on setting line	Mark setting line with chalk line then LX tape
Decide on 2 fixed points (1 + 2)	Mark fixed points on floor, lay end of each measure on each point
Measure from fixed point 1 – point 3	First person find same measurement on tape measure A
Measure from fixed point 2 – 3	Second person find same measurement on tape B
	First and second person pivot both tape measures till they meet at point 3
	Mark with chalk or tape
	Mark up all points this way, then join all marks with coloured LX tape

Ground plan showing flatage for box-set (not to scale):

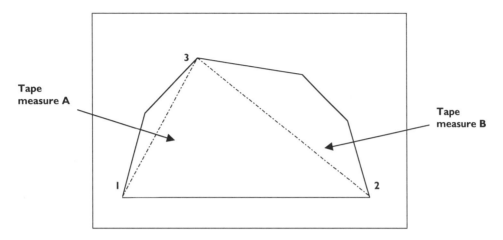

Circles/semi-circles:

- Measure the radius of the circle off the ground plan.
- Mark centre point of the circle on floor.
- Using chalk and string, draw out the circle on the floor.

N.B. Use different colours of LX tape to donate different scenes/sets.

'Are you sure you're using the right side of the scale rule?'

Set up props and furniture in rehearsal room

Once the mark up has been completed, set up all the rehearsal furniture in the space as stipulated by the ground plan. Some companies provide rostra and even flatage to help the performers become familiar with the set.

Lay out all the rehearsal props on various tables situated around the room as neatly as possible. This will encourage tidiness from all at the outset. Wherever possible, set out your props tables as near to how they might be in your performance space, to help the performers get used to the side their props will be going on and off. It is useful to have a separate table for personal props. Be sure to have enough chairs around the room for performers to sit and watch if they are not involved in the action. Provide waste bins, and encourage company to use them.

The DSM should arm herself with a few items the performers may need throughout the rehearsal period:

- Pens/pencils
- Erasers
- First aid kit (containing antiseptic, bandages, plasters, eye wash etc)
- Tissues
- Throat lozenges
- Spare copy of the script etc.

Some rehearsal rooms have a phone, which connects rehearsals to the rest of the production team. This is very handy for emergencies, responding quickly to requests for additional props and the like and getting speedy answers to questions that may arise.

If the rehearsal room is well organised at the beginning of rehearsals this should enable the DSM to keep it tidy and organised throughout the rehearsal period.

Prepare prompt copy

The prompt copy or 'book' is a folder in which all the elements of the performance (cues, calls, blocking etc.) are recorded against the script. Each person will use their own particular method when preparing the prompt copy for rehearsals, but the most important feature must be its accessibility and legibility. Occasionally another member of the team may have to take over the cueing of the show. It is therefore important there should be some uniformity in the way the book is laid out, the methodology of blocking, and how the cues are recorded. As we work through the production process there will be additional information about suggested techniques for the above. Here is one method for preparing your prompt copy before rehearsals begin.

- Photocopy each page of the script onto a single sheet of A4.
- Lay first page of the script on the left-hand side of the folder.
- Lay a blank sheet of A4 on the right hand side.
- Turn over blank page, and lay second page of script on the left again.
- Lay blank sheet on right, and continue until all the script is inserted.

Prepared rehearsal room

This method of laying the script page on the left is useful if you are right handed. It allows you to note the moves more comfortably without have to cross your hand over the script page. The reason for inserting a blank page is to allow for any script changes – eg: cuts and additions – to be inserted without cutting up any blocking or information that may be on the back of a script page. It is a good idea to use reinforcements round the punch-holes to save you losing pages later on!

If you are using graphic notation for blocking, you can prepare the blocking pages before rehearsals begin, using the ground plan.

- Re-draw, or scale down a miniature of the ground plan so it fits on far left column of the blank page.
- Make two copies and lay on page as shown on the diagram below.
- Make as many photocopies of this page as there are script pages, and make up book as described above.

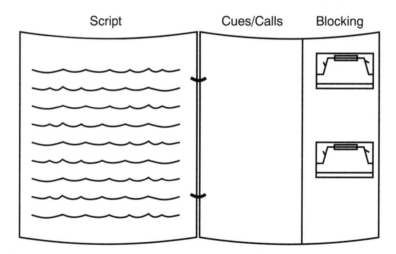

Further information about the production can be inserted at this stage:

- Title page with name of production, writer, director etc.
- Cast list
- Names, addresses and phone numbers of the cast.
- Provisional props list.
- Copy of ground plan for reference purposes.
- Provisional schedule
- Rehearsal schedule
- Availability chart/scene breakdown

You should now be well prepared to receive the company, and begin the rehearsal and build period.

First day of rehearsals

In many Repertory and other types of companies the first day of rehearsals will consist of a *read-through*. Most companies will certainly have a company meeting. To encourage an informal and friendly atmosphere, tea, coffee and sticky buns should be provided. During this meeting all the cast, directors, designers, SMgt team, wardrobe and other members of the production team will get a chance to say hello and begin to get to know each other.

It always amazes me how often one turns up at a read-through to discover many familiar faces. Theatre really is a small world and you can be sure of working with the same people again and again.

If your cast are coming from all over the country it is a good idea to present them with an information pack to assist them in becoming familiar with the town or city they have just arrived in. It should include details of:

- Map of town or city
- Bus/train timetables
- Doctors'/dentists' surgeries
- Recommended pubs, restaurants, clubs, etc.
- Cinemas, churches
- Laundrettes
- Places of interest

The read through

The read-through

1. The director will begin by introducing the company, or may ask them to introduce themselves in turn (usually seated in a big circle).
2. The director then talks about the piece, describes his or her overall vision, reasons for wanting to do this particular piece and outlines the design concepts.
3. Where appropriate the set designer may now present the set model to the company. During this presentation the designer will explain how they arrived at this particular design and run through the movement of the scenery scene by scene. It is extremely helpful to the performers to have this visual representation of the set fixed in their minds before rehearsals begin. It will also assist them to understand the mark up in the rehearsal room.
4. Where appropriate the costume designer will present the costume drawings/plates, and possibly fabric samples.
5. The LX designer may disclose any ideas they have had if they feel it might be useful to the company at this early stage.
6. The company then embark on the read-through.
7. The DSM should be prepared to read in the stage directions and/or any descriptive passages at the director's discretion.
8. The DSM will take a timing of the read-through to give the director a very rough idea of the running time.
9. The SM team should schedule in their props meeting with the director and designer on the first day.

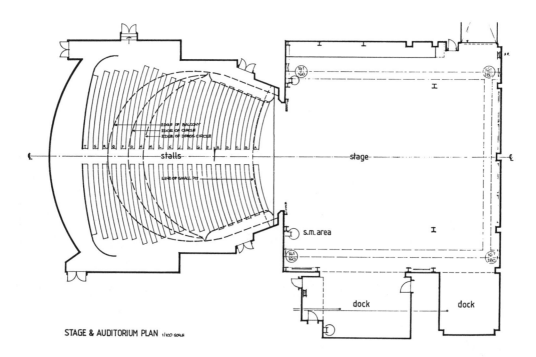

STAGE & AUDITORIUM PLAN 1/100 SCALE

The ground plan

CHAPTER 3

THE REHEARSAL PERIOD

The DSM in rehearsals

The deputy stage manager (DSM on the book) attends all the rehearsal sessions with the company, director, choreographer, musical director and fight director (when appropriate).

The DSM becomes the all-seeing, all-knowing, eyes and ears for the rest of the production team. It is essential that they formulate a fail-safe system for communicating all the information, cuts and additions effectively and accurately to the other production departments.

An experienced DSM will sense instinctively when the performers or director require assistance, and will develop razor sharp hearing to pick up muffled conversations in another corner of the room that may affect any of the production departments.

The DSM's desk in rehearsal

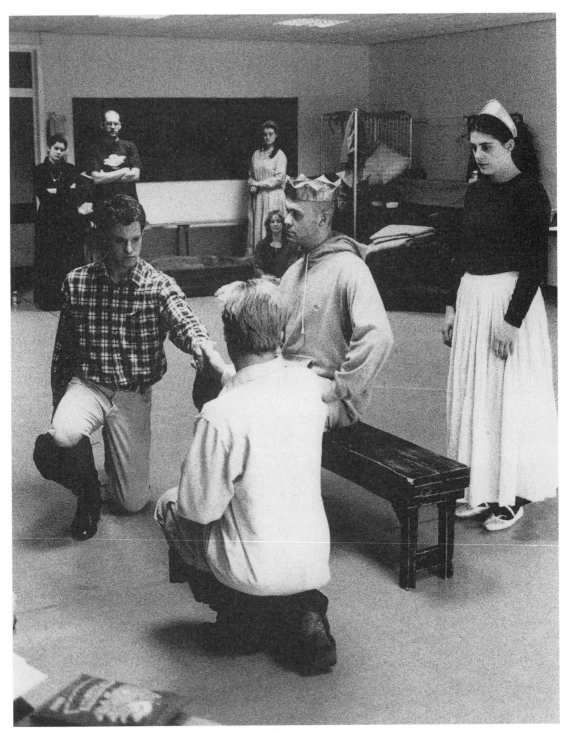

Rehearsals in progress

It is this instinctive awareness and ability to respond quickly and efficiently, which makes the difference between an excellent DSM and a mediocre one. In essence, good DSMs should strive to be proactive rather than reactive.

To operate effectively they need to gain the trust and respect of the company and director. They have to be able to answer, or find the answer to, any questions the company may have relating to any element of the show.

In larger companies the DSM may have an assistant stage manager (ASM) with them in rehearsals to act as a runner, to be responsible for the movement of props and furniture and to contribute to rehearsal notes each day.

It is important to have an empathy with the difficulties and needs of the performers in order to support their work in the rehearsal room.

- Try to socialise and get to know the company as quickly as possible. This will assist you in anticipating their needs.
- Watch out for the performers miming a prop you know nothing about. Often they may work on their characters at home and come in the next day with new ideas, which they haven't discussed with the director. Encourage them to discuss these ideas with the director, to ascertain whether additional props are required.
- Find the right balance between enabling and nursing!
- Be ready to set back quickly and quietly, so the flow of rehearsals is not interrupted.
- Make sure the urn is on for a plentiful supply of tea and coffee, and that there are biscuits to hand!

The DSM's tasks in rehearsals consist of the following:

1. Blocking
2. Prompting
3. Rehearsal notes
4. Rehearsal calls
5. Contact sheet
6. Setting plots
7. Running plots

1. Blocking

Blocking is the recording of the performers' entrances, exits, moves, gestures, pace, use of props etc against the script. This serves as a daily reference for the performers and director during rehearsals, and is a record of the moves. There are two types of blocking used in theatre: graphic and shorthand notation. Personally, I prefer to use a mixture of both.

Graphic:

The moves are recorded on a reduced, simplified ground plan, using the following symbols to represent the movement:

○	-	Position of character (stationary)
Ⓜ	-	Character symbol
→	-	Arrow indicates direction of travel
→₂	-	Number indicates position of move against the script

The diagram below shows the following move in graphic form:

Malcolm enters from upstage right, walks downstage right towards the table, crosses stage left to chair, and sits.

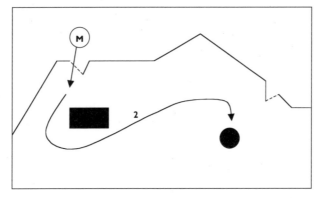

Shorthand:

Most theatre practitioners use a common language when referring to different areas of the stage. The stage can be divided into nine areas, as shown in the table below.

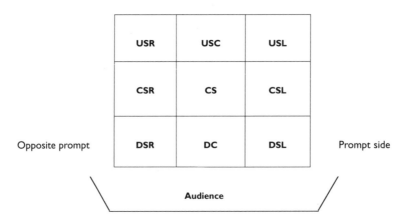

These are the most commonly used symbols in shorthand, and personal preferences will dictate the rest.

Key to most common symbols and abbreviations:

USR	-	Upstage right	**USL**	-	Upstage left
CR	-	Centre right	**CL**	-	Centre left
DSR	-	Downstage right	**DSL**	-	Downstage left
X	-	Crosses	↓	-	Sits down
En	-	Enters	↑	-	Stands
Ex	-	Exits		-	Goes upstairs
⌣•	-	Short pause		-	Goes downstairs
⌢•	-	Long pause			

Thus the following move: *Malcolm enters from upstage right, walks downstage right towards the table, crosses stage left to chair, and sits...* could be shown in shorthand like this:

Ⓜ en. USR, X DSR→T 1. X SL→Ch.1 +↓

Here is an example of how we can combine both graphic and shorthand to notate the following moves:

Malcolm enters upstage right, walks downstage to right of table, crosses in front of it then walks over to chair and sits down.
He picks up the newspaper and reads it.
He stands and runs out of centre stage left door.

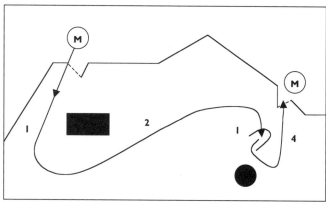

2. Ⓜ ↓
3. Ⓜ **reads newspapers**
4. Ⓜ **runs**

Remember to note the corresponding position of the moves on the script page, as in the diagram below.

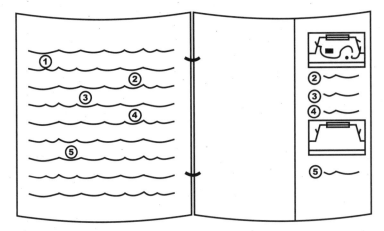

For those trying this out for the first time, use a soft pencil and equip yourself with a good eraser. Invariably the moves will change throughout the rehearsal process, which means lots of rubbing out and re-blocking. When you get to the bottom of a page start re-numbering the moves from 1 again on the top of the next page.

If the play is in the round, use the numerals of a clock face to note the performers' positions.

2. Prompting

A 'prompt' is a word or line given to the performer by the DSM when they 'dry' (forget their lines). It is essential that the DSM is able to give a prompt effectively, so the flow of the performer's speech and train of thought is aided and not abetted.

Every performer will have a method of asking for a prompt. Some say 'line', 'prompt' or 'yes!' Others will just pause and look concerned. Some may even utter a range of expletives under their breath. Once the DSM knows the performers well, they will often be able to anticipate the need for a prompt.

Effective prompting

- Project the line clearly and loudly.
- Know how much of the line is required.
- Know when a prompt is needed (or whether it is a dramatic pause.)
- Keep your finger on the line of script with one hand, if you are blocking with the other. (It is easy to be caught out if you are asked for a prompt, and are concentrating on blocking.)
- The better aquainted with the script you are, the quicker the response time will be.
- As you begin to get to grips with each performer's timing and characterisations, it will become easier to anticipate their need for a prompt.

Vocal projection

Be aware of your own vocal potential. It is extremely frustrating for a performer to have to ask for a prompt twice as they couldn't hear the line the first time round. I used to hum to myself on the way to rehearsals in the morning, or even join in the performers vocal warm up, to help loosen up the vocal chords. Posture while sitting on the book can affect your ability to project effectively.

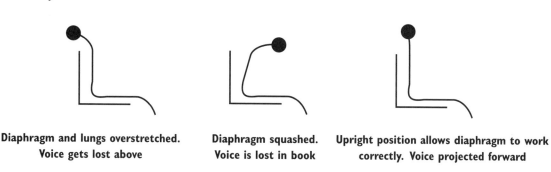

Diaphragm and lungs overstretched. Voice gets lost above   **Diaphragm squashed. Voice is lost in book**   **Upright position allows diaphragm to work correctly. Voice projected forward**

3. Rehearsal notes

One of the main functions of the DSM is to relay all additions, cuts and changes from the rehearsal room to rest of the production team. The most effective and widely used method is rehearsal notes.

At the end of each rehearsal the DSM will write up a list of all the notes that have been made during that rehearsal session pertaining to all the other production departments. As this is the main line of communication between the company and the production team it is vital that the DSM makes detailed and accurate notes throughout rehearsals. It is beneficial to all concerned if the DSM can check through all the notes at the end of the day with the director. At this point the director may wish to give more detail about additions, or decide to cut certain items that were vaguely discussed earlier.

Most companies use a template (some have it on disk) which can be typed up or processed. On completion each day the DSM will photocopy the rehearsal notes and post them round every department. It is important that even though there may not be any notes for a particular department on that day, they will still get a copy. This ensures that each department is aware of the changes in other departments, which might indirectly affect them.

Wherever possible, often dependant on time, the DSM will meet with the stage manager to run through the notes for that day, discussing the priorities and problem items that may come up. It is essential the DSM gives detailed and accurate information to each department:

- When describing a new prop – eg: a sandwich – make sure you have already asked the performer whether they like the filling, and if not what they would like instead. Check with the director the quantity required for each performance.

REHEARSAL NOTES

Show: 'Pantoland'

No: 4

Date: 15 November

Signed: DSM

SM/Props

1. Can we have the flying teddy in rehearsals as soon as possible please, so that the performers can try it with the action?
2. We will need two more giant ice creams for Scene 3.
3. A red toadstool has been requested for scene 5. Liase with props maker.
4. 2 x bags of silver glitter to be thrown by the fairy is needed for scene 10.
5. A large gold cushion with tassels is required for the king in scene 10.
6. Can we have three more copies of the score for 'Rainbow' to rehearse with on Tuesday?

Set

1. The upstage treads in rehearsals are proving difficult for the fight sequence in scene 2. Would the designer please check that the dimensions of the actual treads are wider before going ahead with the build?
2. The dames cossie in scene 4 may be too wide for the DSL exit; please check.
3. We may need handholds in the counter for ease of striking. SMgt liase.

LX

1. A practical storm lantern is required for the keeper in scene 6.
2. The fairy lights will need to be struck for scene 7.
3. The director would like a quick chat re the transformation scene. Could the designer pop into rehearsals at the end of the morning session tomorrow?

Sound

1. May we have a cock crowing sound effect at the top of scene 5 please?
2. Are there enough radio mics for the keeper also to have one in scene 4?
3. The horse and cart effect is to last for at least 10 seconds.

Wardrobe

1. May we have the rehearsal cossie for the dame (scene 5) a.s.a.p. please?
2. 5 x oriental fans are required for the ladies (scene 8).
3. Please advise how high the matron's wig is in scene 8. We are unsure of her USR exit.

CC: Production HoDs, Director, Set, Costume, LX, Sound Designers, Choreographer, MD.

- If a sound cue has been added check with the director the exact requirements of the sound effect. How long does it run for? Does it fade in or out?
- If a piece of scenery is worrying the director, perhaps in terms of practicality, then get as much information as possible about alternative ideas. Suggest that the director meets with the designer to discuss it in more detail.
- If a new piece of costume has been requested by a performer always double check that the director is in agreement. Then elicit information as to its colour, shape and size. And again, suggest that the director and designer discuss it further.
- If a practical lamp is requested of the LX department, check where it is to be situated and during which scene is it needed. Then liase with SMgt as to who will prop it.

See opposite for an example of rehearsal notes *(templates, see page 139)*:

4. Rehearsal calls

The DSM is responsible for posting the call sheet *(for example see below, template page 138)* on a specified notice board each day. This informs not only the performers but the production team what is going to be rehearsed and where the following day. The DSM will discuss the calls with the director at the end of rehearsals, then type or process them for distribution. The DSM should liase with each department to ensure the calls are manageable (eg: wardrobe fittings).

Time	Company	Call	Location
10 am	Ms Wood Ms Scholar Ms Spencer	Scene 1 & 2	Reh. room 1
11am	Ms Sate to join		
10.30 am	Mr Nairn Mr Queripel	Fight scene p 21	Reh. room 2
11.30 am	Ms Maclean Ms Bruce	Dance reh.	Stduio 2
1 pm	LUNCH		
2 pm	Full company	Music call 'Only You'	Reh. room 1
3 pm	Full company	Photo call 'Tableau'	Studio 2
3.30 pm	Mr Wild Ms Christine	Wardrobe fitting	Wardrobe

There are many different types of calls:

- Rehearsing specific scenes
- Music call
- Dance call
- Stage fight call
- Wardrobe fittings
- Press call
- Photo call

Many of these calls could be in different spaces so the location should be stated.

To assist the DSM write up the calls quickly each day, many use a chart called a scene breakdown. This shows at a glance who is in which scene.

Availability chart:

Character	Act 1, scene 1	1.2	1.3	Act 2, scene 1	2.2	Act 3
Talitha		X		X		
Hamish			X	X	X	
Sandra		X				
Nick		X		X		X
Jimmy	X				X	
Florrie	X					
Dougal	X			X		X
Gaynor		X	X	X		X
Roland			X		X	X
Jill			X			X

5. Contact sheet

At the beginning of the rehearsal period the DSM compiles a list of the company's names, addresses and phone numbers. If a member of the company is late for rehearsals, or fails to appear at all it is up to the DSM to contact them to find out what the problem is, and to notify the director.

- Hand round a sheet during the read-through for each member of the company to fill in.
- Compile all the names, addresses and phone numbers.
- Give copies to the director, stage manager and put a copy in the book.

'What do you mean, 'make the tea'?!'

6. Setting Plots

The DSM should begin to compile the setting plot early on in the rehearsal process to be finalised during pre-production week.

The setting plot refers to the position of all the props, furniture, dressing and sometimes elements of the set at the top of the show (where every item should begin). The DSM will begin to collate this information throughout rehearsals. It is often necessary to have a little diagram of each scene showing the setting of props and furniture to facilitate accurate setting up of each scene during the rehearsal process. The director may not rehearse each scene in order, hence the need for separate lists or diagrams for each scene. However, once the company begins to do runs of the play the DSM will build the master setting plot, describing where all the items start from at the top of the show.

It is paramount that all items are recorded precisely and accurately.

- The performer needs to know each item will be in exactly the same place every performance. Many performers use what is called 'muscle memory' which enables them to locate a chair, pen, phone etc without having to look round for it. This ability enhances the audience's belief that this character has, for example, inhabited this particular room for ten years. If the SMgt team have not set that particular chair or pen in exactly the same place the performer may misjudge the position, resulting in the performer missing it, and throwing the flow of the performance.

- The setting plot must be neat, and easy to follow. There may be different people setting up and checking, so it should be accessible to anyone.
- The neater the backstage props tables, the easier it is to set up and check, and the easier it is for the actors to find their props during the show. Indeed this may also encourage them to replace the props back neatly after use, if they have not been left onstage.
- A fail safe method to check that all items have been included on the setting plot is to cross reference the props list with the setting plot, at which point any omissions should be spotted.
- The sooner the DSM has collated the setting plot the sooner the rest of the SMgt team can assist with the daily setting up of rehearsals.
- If elements of the set are different between the end of one show and the top of the next show (doors, windows etc) then include this information on the setting plot. The movement of props, furniture and set during the actual show will be recorded on the running plot.
- I have always tried to encourage my DSMs to use the word processor for their lists and diagrams, as this looks more professional and is usually easier to read.

Layout of setting plots

The setting plot should be divided into different sections depending on the layout of your theatre or performance space. They could be split as follows:

Onstage
Backstage
Personals

If there are pieces of furniture with many props set on or in them, then it may be necessary to do a separate diagram showing the detail.

Onstage setting plot

Draw a diagram of the set *(see opposite, top)*, furniture and props then number all items accordingly.

Backstage props

As the props tables backstage will be marked up with tape and labelled, there is no need to do a diagram *(see page 84)*. A list of the props required in this area is sufficient. This list should contain as much detail as possible. When you are collating this list, imagine the person setting up does not know the show at all. This should encourage you to put in the relevant detail. If you are touring the show then lay white paper on the props table and mark it out. This can then be rolled up and re-laid in each venue, allowing continuity.

Onstage

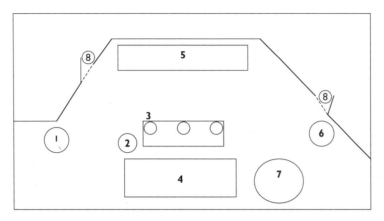

1. Round table with aspidistra plant
2. Oval table with book and spectacles
3. Sofa with 3 x blue cushions
4. Large cream rug
5. Sideboard, with:
    a) green vase
    b) statue
    c) rose bowl
    d) 3 x books
6. Round table and candlestick telephone
7. Table, with:
    a) flute
    b) Gladstone bag
    c) manuscript
    d) teacup and saucer (empty)
8. Doors shut; curtains closed

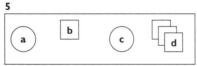

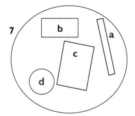

Backstage

- 2 x glasses of white wine (half full)
- 3 x folded white napkins (ironed)
- 5 x sponge cakes on white bread plate

- Black briefcase.   Inside:

	top	mobile phone
	mid	10 sheets typed reports
	bottom	2 x car magazines
	pocket	3 x black pens (practical)

- 3 x books :   *The Works of Shakespeare*
    Tales of the City
    Knots and Crosses

- 2 x newspapers: *The Scotsman* (folded once showing photo of Hussein)
    The Independent (folded twice showing crossword)

- Black teapot (empty)

- Flask of hot black tea

- Tray: sugar bowl with white sugar
  milk jug with inch of milk
  3 x white cups and saucers
  3 x teaspoons

- Magnifying glass

- Photo of grandfather

Personals

These are small props set in the dressing room at the top of the show and should be listed under the performer's name.

Ms White: Handbag: car keys, hanky, lipstick, purse with 3 x 50p coins
Gold crucifix
Gold watch

Mr Jones: Wallet: 2 x £5 notes, photo of Jess, 2 x receipts, dressing
Pkt. *Silk Cut* with 3 x cigs
Box of matches (1 preset)
Bottle of 10 x pills in bottom left pocket of blue jacket

7. Running plot

This refers to the list of tasks the SMgt team does during the running of the show. The DSM will collate this list during the rehearsal process as the director decides what will happen and when.

This list should include:

- Beginners
- Scene changes
- Paging doors and blacks
- Handing props to performers if they don't have time to get them from the props table
- Food preparation
- Live sound cues, eg: door slams, bells, crashes etc
- Cueing performers onstage if necessary

The DSM will try to record all tasks no matter how small. This list must also be neat and accurate in case someone new has to take over during the show.

To assist the team's efficiency during the technical rehearsal, the more detail given at the outset, the easier it will be to run the technical effectively. The DSM will issue a master running plot, which the team divides up among themselves. It is then the responsibility of each team member to compile their own running plot after the cuts and additions sustained during production week. The list should carry the following information:

- Number of cue
- Page number of cue as it relates to the script
- Concise description of the task/cue
- Line or input point of cue
- Backstage position for executing cue

Example of running plot:

Cue	Page	Description	Input	Position
1	Beginners	Ms Shapcot Ms Maclean Mr Wild		USL DSR
2	3	Hand Ms Maclean axe	'over to you Alan'	DSR
3	5	Pour tea from flask into teapot	As Hetty exits	USL
4	10	Page blacks for wedding party	As Amy approaches	DSR
5	14	Doorslam	'Who is that....'	USR
6	18	Rattle crash box	' Arrrrrgggh…'	USR

Scene Changes

If the scene change is small, involving only a few props, then it is reasonable to list the items on a list as above. However many scene changes may involve changing from one setting to another, or even a time shift. If set, furniture and props have to be struck and reset the use of diagrams comes in handy here also. I have found the following diagrams (a before and after) very useful in containing all the necessary information in an accessible format *(see page 50)*. It can state who does what during the change, and in what order.

- Strike – To remove an item from the stage to offstage
- Set – To bring an item from offstage to onstage
- Reset – To move an item onstage to another position onstage

Production meetings

Production/progress meetings are generally held once a week throughout the rehearsal/build period. This affords the opportunity for all the department heads, designers and the director, who may be working in different locations, to come together regularly.

The main objective is:

- To discuss changes, alterations and additions
- To share problems
- To agree on deadlines
- To monitor progress

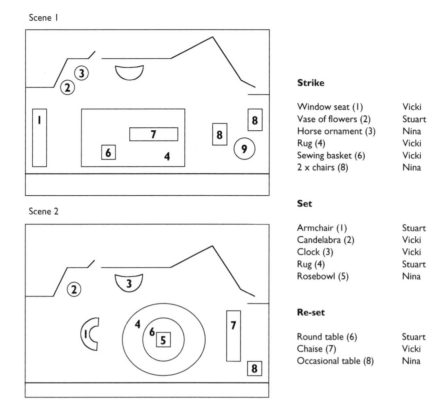

Strike

Window seat (1)	Vicki
Vase of flowers (2)	Stuart
Horse ornament (3)	Nina
Rug (4)	Vicki
Sewing basket (6)	Vicki
2 x chairs (8)	Nina

Set

Armchair (1)	Stuart
Candelabra (2)	Vicki
Clock (3)	Vicki
Rug (4)	Stuart
Rosebowl (5)	Nina

Re-set

Round table (6)	Stuart
Chaise (7)	Vicki
Occasional table (8)	Nina

The production manager will chair the meeting. His/her role is:

- To instigate discussion
- To motivate and drive the meeting
- To be concerned with process as well as content
- To protect the weak and control the strong

The DSM takes the minutes, then ensures that they are typed up and distributed in good time. As with any meeting it is important to:

- Listen actively
- Give direct replies
- Question critically
- Avoid interrupting
- Refrain from distracting behaviour
- Summarise progress at regular intervals
- Be supportive

CHAPTER 4

PROPS MANAGEMENT

The process

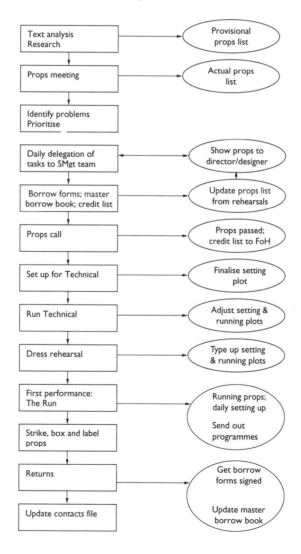

Text analysis
Research
→ Provisional props list

Props meeting
→ Actual props list

Identify problems
Prioritise

Daily delegation of tasks to SMgt team
← Show props to director/designer

Borrow forms; master borrow book; credit list
Update props list from rehearsals

Props call
→ Props passed; credit list to FoH

Set up for Technical
→ Finalise setting plot

Run Technical
→ Adjust setting & running plots

Dress rehearsal
→ Type up setting & running plots

First performance: The Run
→ Running props; daily setting up

Send out programmes

Strike, box and label props

Returns
→ Get borrow forms signed

Update master borrow book

Update contacts file

Textual analysis

The first task when approaching a play is to get a copy of the script as early as possible and read through it at least twice. Once you have absorbed the general ambience and feel of the piece, go through it slowly section by section and pull out all the props and furniture that are mentioned or even implied.

Some scripts have a props list at the back, but it is not wise to use this as the basis for your provisional props list as it may not be accurate. It is necessary to make a note of any live sound effects, as the DSM will be required to replicate these in rehearsals (rehearsal bells, phones, etc). Once you have made a detailed list of all the props from your reading of the script, this becomes your 'provisional props list', which the team will use to gather rehearsal props and furniture.

Research

At this stage it is necessary to have a brief discussion with the director and designer to check in which period the play is going to be set. Once you have this information, you can set about researching the period, the country, and the historical background of the piece. Most colleges and theatres have a small stock of reference books which may give you a good insight into the look of the props and furniture, eg: *Millers Antiques Guide (see chapter 13)*. If not, all libraries will provide ample reference guides. The Internet is also an invaluable source of references.

It is very important to get a feel for the period, and an understanding of the visual style of the production, as it will save a lot of time when propping if you instinctively know that a certain item is just right.

Props meeting

Before rehearsals begin and you actually start propping, sit down with the director and designer and go through your provisional props and furniture list item by item to illicit as much information as you can (set aside at least an hour for this). For example:

Prop A: cushion
Question: What size, shape, colour, weight?

Prop B: bottle of beer
Question: Is it practical? Is it opened on-stage or off? How much of it gets consumed? Does it need to be a specific make? Is the label seen? (This would mean getting a laser copy from the manufacturer if it is a period item).

Prop C: table
Question: Exact dimensions? How is it used? Does anyone stand or sit on it? What shape, colour, etc?

Those of you who have worked a few shows will know only too well how hard it is to find time with the director once rehearsals are under way, so taking time at this meeting will save time later on in the process. You will also be able to check on any cuts and/ or additions the director has decided on during his own research.

This collated information now becomes your 'accurate props list'.

Example of accurate props list (template on page 140)

Props List

Page	Item	Source	Rehearsal	Actual	Designer Pass	Director Pass	Props Call Pass
I	2 x wicker baskets	Stock	x	x	x	x	
2	6 x food parcels	Make	x	x	x	x	
4	10 x beer bottles (pract)	Stock/make labels	x				
4	2 x daily newspapers	Hire/ photocopy	x				
4	Pair of reading spectacles	Borrow/ opticians	x	x		x	
4	4 x beer glasses	Stock	x	x	x	x	
6	6 x dinner plates	Borrow/ department stores	x				
6	6 x knives	Borrow/ department stores	x				
6	6 x forks	Borrow/ department stores	x				
6	6 x spoons	Borrow/ department stores	x				
6	6 x side plates	Borrow/ department stores	x				
6	6 x butter knives	Borrow/ department stores	x				
16	6 x napkins	Borrow/ department stores	x				
16	Cat ornament	Borrow	x				
16	Blue vase	Borrow/ antique shops	x				
16	Bunch of red carnations	Donations/ florists	x				
16	Tissue paper for flowers	Donations/ florists	x				
	4 x cigarettes/ night	Donations					
20	Cigarette case	Stock	x	x	x	x	
20	Table lighter	Borrow/ tobacconist	x				
22	Bottle of gin (pract)	Stock/ make label	x				
22	2 x gin glasses	Stock	x	x		x	

Identify problems and prioritise

Once you have compiled your accurate props list, spend a little time working out which props and furniture you deem to be the most difficult to find, and which will take the longest to make. These are the items that you should start on first. Prioritise your list, and try to work out how much time each prop will take, always thinking ahead to the deadline, which is the Props Call. The deadline might be even earlier than that if it is something that a performer needs to spend more time working with in rehearsals.

Daily delegation of tasks

Always meet with the team at the start of each propping day, to decide who is the most appropriate person for each task *(See* Delegation, *chapter 8)*. This is most effectively done over a cup of tea! Once the day's work has been planned and delegated, the team will head off in various directions to begin propping.

'So let me get this right. You borrow this 18th century mirror, and in return I get a credit in the programme, a complimentary ticket and a promise?'

On retrieving an actual prop, find the director and designer as soon as possible to get it passed. There is nothing more frustrating, and potentially time wasting, than letting a collection of props sit in a cupboard for days only to find that they do not get the approval of the director and designer. There is also the added benefit of ticking off the passed column on a regular basis, so you can see at a glance what progress is being made. (Separated columns enable this process)

Borrow Form, Master Borrow Book, Credits List

Example of a borrow form, for template see page 145.

Borrow Form		
Date: 15/1/00		
On loan to: The Gateway Theatre Edinburgh		
On loan from: Cubble Antiques The Square Edinburgh 112-0012		
Items	**Condition**	**Value**
Victorian vase	Excellent	£72
Scrap book	Cover damaged	£15
Set of 6 x plates (with Gold Edge)	I small chip in I x plate	£35
Cigarette case	Good	£22
Date for return: 15/2/00		
Signature of recipient: *(signature)* (D. Howard)		
Actual return date:		
Confirmation of return (print name):		

It is vital to any company, no matter how small, to have well presented borrow forms.

- They instil a sense of trust with the person/company from whom you are borrowing.
- They allow you to keep an accurate record of all items borrowed, and to note their condition.
- On return of props you ask the person/company to sign for the safe return of their property, and keep this as a record. This is especially necessary if there is a regular turnover of staff, or the show is a one-off, as it allows the responsible person to give proof that returns were done.

Master Borrow Book *(see page 91)*

- On return to base with prop and borrow/hire form, fill in the master borrow book.
- This keeps information on all borrows, donations and hires in one place.
- It provides excellent reference material for future shows.
- It provides a collated account for returns.

Credits List *(for template, see page 143)*

Fill in details for your acknowledgements on a daily basis so when the programme deadline comes along, your list is already collated.

Props List Update

At the end of a working day, most teams will get together (if time allows) and report back on progress made. This allows the SM to tick off any found props and furniture, and to read through the rehearsal notes to adjust the master props list. Most days there will be cuts and additions resulting from the creative process during rehearsals, and the props list should be updated on a daily basis. If a particular item is proving to be troublesome or beyond the budget, this should be flagged up with the director or production manager as soon as possible and alternative solutions identified.

The cycle of: meet, delegate, retrieve, seek approval, fill in necessary paperwork and update list continues on through the production period until all props and furniture are found. The goal that should be in mind throughout this period is the 'props call'.

Props call

The team will spread out all the props neatly, usually scene by scene, and take the director and designer through each item to double check they are all present and correct. Once you have confirmation of which items are being used in the show, the credits list can be handed over to Front of House for the programme, adhering to the credit deadline *(details page 69)*.

Set up for technical

During the session before the technical is due to start, the stage management team will need some time on-stage to clear, tidy and make safe all areas on and off stage, and to set out all the props, furniture and dressing *(for more details, see page 78)*. This is done using setting plots provided by the DSM on the book.

It is often the case that once the team has set up, the setting plot may need to be adjusted to allow for differences between the rehearsal room and the actual set.

The technical

The SM and the DSM on the book will have prepared their running plots prior to the technical, so the actual running of the show is already worked out (ie: who does what and when). It is now the responsibility of the team to ensure a capable, relaxed attitude to all activities during the technical, which will help inspire confidence with the performers and the director.

During the technical any alterations to the setting/running plots should be made immediately (never rely on memory) and at the end of the session the team should find time to re-write their own plots *(details page 80)*.

Dress rehearsal(s)

This is the first opportunity for the team to check that their running plots work in real time, and that setting plots are accurate *(details page 82)*.

First performance and the run

Between each dress rehearsal, and usually after the first few performances, there will be notes sessions, taken by either the director and/or the production manager. The SMgt team will finish off the last few jobs on the props and furniture, and adjust their setting and running plots accordingly.

At this point the show is more or less set, and the teams responsibility is to ensure the show runs smoothly.

Once the run is under way, and if one is employed for a season of plays, the team falls into a routine for the show call, and will start concentrating all their energies on propping the next show during the day *(details page 85)*.

Final performance and the strike

During the final performance the SMgt team begin to strike all the props to a suitable storage area. Be careful to ensure the struck prop does not get used again later on in the show. I have fallen foul of this once – a scary moment not just for me, but for the performer concerned *(details page 89–90)*!

Returns

On the first working day after the run ends, the team return all the props and furniture to their respective owners. Don't forget that it is vital to get a signature on the borrow form as proof of return. Once all props, furniture and dressing have been returned the master borrow book can then be filled in *(see page 90)*.

Update contacts file

It is in your own, as well as your company's, interest to keep the contacts file up to date. It will prove invaluable when propping future shows. Most professional stage managers have their own contacts book that they take from job to job. There are only so many places where you can find some items, and many contacts are nation wide. Keep your own records as you will use them again, no matter where you are working.

PROPS AND PROPPING: Types of props

Rehearsal

These are items that can be found usually in stock, and are provided for rehearsal purposes only. It is necessary to provide something that will represent every item on the props and furniture list, so that the actors get used to working with them. Ensure these items are roughly the same size and weight as the actual prop (eg: a suitcase is filled with old blankets if there is to be clothing in the actual one).

Actual

The pieces of furniture or prop that you deem correct for the period, and that fulfils the requirements of that scene. Once you have found an 'actual' try to get it passed by the director and designer as soon as possible. Many designers have a very clear idea what they are looking for, and in order to succeed it is important to try to bond with the designer's visual interpretation of the play. You may have to proffer a few variations on a theme before the designer approves it. Don't lose heart, ask the designer to draw a sketch if the description is not clear enough.

It is also true that although a prop or piece of furniture is absolutely correct in terms of period, it may not sit well with the rest of the set and dressing, therefore one must rely on the designer's overview, and go with their judgement.

Practical

A prop that is used in a practical way, ie: a knife that has to cut bread; a gun that is fired; a bell that rings.

Many practical props require consideration when used in a show context. There are strict laws adhering to the use of firearms *(see chapter 10)*. The use of weapons or knives should be strictly controlled, and made as safe as possible. Many companies hire a fight director if there are scenes with stage fighting.

At this point it is entirely relevant to mention that wonderful product, burnt sugar (available from chemists). If you need to mock up wine, sherry, tea, coffee, brandy or various other beverages this is a *must*. A few drops of this product will colour water, is totally tasteless, and is made from sugar – which most performers will cope with.

Furniture store

Comestibles

Props which are eaten or used up every night.

- Food: Make sure the performer can eat the foodstuffs.
- Cigarettes: Does the performer smoke? There are herbal alternatives.
- Torn up paper: How much will you need for the run?

It is important to work out at the outset how many of each item you will need for the whole run. This will affect the budget, and will save time and money if you buy in bulk. NB: If naked flames or pyrotechnics are used during the show all paper, soft furnishings, drapes and often parts of the set must be fire-proofed.

Personals

A prop that is set in the dressing room at the top of the show, as opposed to a prop which the performer uses personally and is set on the props table (this description often gets confused). For example: watches, jewellery, handbags, cigarettes, lighters, canes etc. These props will be either laid out at the performer's dressing table area, or set in their costume.

It is the responsibility of the DSM to go round the dressing rooms at the half- hour call to check the personals. It is then the responsibility of the performers to bring the prop to the stage.

Set dressing

This term applies to all items of props and furniture that are not actually used during the show, and remain in one place throughout any given scene.
They add a sense of reality to a set, and can make a room look lived in.
Examples: pictures on a wall, superfluous tables and chairs, vases, ornaments, books.

When discussing the props list with the designer at the beginning of the propping process, check what amount – and type – of set dressing they require. It is often the case that the number of items on your set dressing list can be as long as the actual props list (depending on the type and style of set).

Performer proof

Wherever possible, ensure that all props are as sturdy as possible. If something can get broken, it will! Think ahead and provide non-breakable items if there is a choice. Where crockery and glasses are being used always have spares at the ready (a performer's nerves can get the better of him/her sometimes).

Interpretation

How one item on your props list, for example a picture, can be interpreted:

1. Rehearsal prop   An empty wooden frame
2. Actual prop   Scottish landscape water colour, 5 ft by 6 ft
3. Practical prop   The above picture which has to fall off the wall.
4. Comestible prop   A picture which gets ripped each night.
5. Personal prop   A locket with a picture inside.
6. Set dressing   The water colour which remains on the wall throughout and is not referred to by the performer or is part of the action.

Soft furnishings store

Methods of procurement

How you go about procuring all the props and furniture will very much depend on your budget, and the size of the company you are working for.

- *Small scale/college/amateur company* – SMgt will make or borrow most of the required items.
- *Middle size company* – SMgt will borrow, hire and buy, assisted by the design team, and often props makers.
- *Large company* – Props buyers will buy – or hire – all items, while the props makers will look after all the makes. SMgt in this instance are required to issue the lists, keep the above departments informed of all cuts, and additions, and are mainly responsible for running rehearsals, and company care.

Assuming that your company is small to middle scale, here are some pointers to procuring props, furniture and set dressing.

Stock

Always check your own props store first, you may be surprised at what is hidden away in the depths of some dark corner. I've found the best way to keep a check on all your own stock is to regularly tidy the store. This also saves time when you need an item quickly, as all items should be easy to see.

Props store

Borrow

There is an art to borrowing, and this comes with experience and confidence. Some stage managers have a natural ability, and some may do better to delegate the task to someone else.

Imagine you are a detective, and have faith that you will find the item eventually. All it takes are research skills, determination and patience. When you begin to search for a particular prop, keep a note of all the places, and people you have tried in case you have to hand over to someone else.

SMgt personnel spend many hours on the phone trying to locate the required props and furniture, and all develop their own phone technique.

- Introduce yourself. Be clear, positive and friendly.
- Tell them about the show, and explain your needs.
- Try to find common ground to put them at ease.
- Mention your tiny budgets, and how you would like to borrow their item.
- Tell them that you have advertising in the programme, and comp tickets to offer in return, and assure them that all items will be insured.
- You will be continually surprised at how kind and helpful most people are.
- If that particular person/company can't actually supply the item, they may be able to suggest where you try next. Always ask for further advice. This is where the detective work comes in: one clue leads to the next, and the next...

Here are a few examples of the 'props detective' at work:

Prop required: *The Times* newspaper from a specific date.

1. Phone *The Times* who produce birthday issues for specific dates. Look in the paper, call directory enquiries or talking pages for the number.
2. Hire the edition you need from a hire-company for a week, and photocopy it onto newsprint. Look in Spotlight's *Contacts* book.

3. Make up the heading on a word processor, then photocopy it, with the rest of any relevant period paper onto newsprint. Size of broadsheet will differ depending on the period, the country etc.

Prop required: Silver Georgian Teapot.

1. Look through *Yellow Pages* for all antique shops in your area.
2. Either phone them up or, if you feel it more appropriate, visit in person.
3. Try hotels. They may have reproductions.
4. Try catering suppliers.

Prop required: American wrapped white bread.

1. Ask around for any ex-pat Americans in the area, and see if their mum could send a few bags over!
2. Phone American restaurants and get the name of their suppliers; they may be able to supply them.
3. Try American military bases or American-owned businesses.
4. Try and find someone friendly at the American Embassy. Above all, keep asking for more advice and more leads.

Prop required: period radio

1. Begin with a shop that sells these types of items.
2. If they can't help, then ask them for the number of any local club or organisation. Try and get a copy of their newsletter.
3. Follow the club route and you should find a helpful enthusiast who will be more than willing to assist you.

One word of warning: NEVER borrow anything that the owner has described as having sentimental value, such as a family heirloom or something incredibly valuable. You cannot absolutely guarantee that it will not get damaged. It can be very stressful for both the owner and also for the stage manager who has to return the broken goods. I speak from experience on this!

Makes

• Where this is the appropriate action, cost the materials, then ask the designer/scenic painters for advice and possible assistance.
• If the company has a props maker, then pass all the relevant information on to him or her.
• See the section on 'Further Reading' (chapter 13) for information on props making literature.

Hire

• If your budget will allow, then telephone round the many and various companies that hire out props and furniture to theatrical, television and film companies *(see Spotlight's Contacts for details)*.

- You will also find a few antique shops that will be happy to hire to theatre companies, usually for 10% of the borrowed item's value per week, as long as you can guarantee its insurance.

Buy

- Scrounge first, buy later!

Budget control

The production manager controls the overall production budget. Each Head of Department (HoD) is allocated a top figure that they have to stay within. In order to control spending effectively and to make the most of the budget one is given it is necessary to keep a running total and account for every penny spent. Many companies now use computer software such as Microsoft Excel in order to achieve this. Put simply, most companies have three types of spending:

1. Petty cash
2. Order forms
3. Transfers

Petty cash

HoD's hold a float of a given amount of cash. This can be spent at the discretion of the HoD. For every item bought receipts are kept and details of what the item is, how much it was, the date, the department, who bought it, and the production are written on the back.

Once a week the HoD will fill in a petty cash form, attach the receipts to it and hand it to the finance department to be reimbursed. Thus the float is topped up weekly *(see petty cash template on page 141)*.

The HoD should also account for this spending on a budget analysis sheet, using relevant columns to state who spent the money and getting the initials of the buyer when monies have been reimbursed. For an example of a budget analysis sheet, see below *(template on page 144)*.

Order forms

If an item can be bought by ordering straight from the company then the HoD will fill in the order form. This form can either be posted out to the company and the goods delivered, or can be taken to the company if the goods are being picked up. Copies of the order form should go to Finance, the PM, and then be accounted for on the HoD's budget analysis sheet.

Transfers

If interdepartmental spending occurs, ie: the SMgt team use a tin of paint from the paint shop, then the cost can be refunded using a transfer system. A transfer form is completed instructing finance to move a given amount from one department to another. This transaction happens on paper only and no actual money is exchanged. A copy of the transfer form is given to Finance, the PM, and to the departments involved in the transaction. The HoD will account for this on the budget analysis sheet.

In this way all spending is accounted for and both the HoD and the PM know exactly what has been spent from day to day.

Example of a budget analysis sheet (see page 144 for template):

Budget Analysis Sheet

Show: *The Basement*   **Date: 1-3-00**
Dept: Stage Management   **Budget: £850**

Date	No	Item	Who	Initials	PC/OF/T	Cost	Balance
1-3-00	1	Stationary	GP		PC	12.56	837.44
2-3-00	2	Felt	AW		PC	6.50	830.94
2-3-00	3	Spray paint	AS		PC	14.23	816.71
2-3-00	4	2 x glasses	GP		PC	15.20	801.51
2-3-00	5	Marker pens	SM		PC	4.68	796.83
5-3-00	23	5m material			Order	27.40	769.43
6-3-00	24	5 litres fire proofing			Order	13.73	755.70
6-3-00	25	25m braid			Order	7.22	748.48
8-3-00	1	2 x tins paint			Transfer	12.45	736.08

CHAPTER 5

PRE-PRODUCTION WEEK

During the last week of the rehearsal period (pre-production week) there are four main activities which assist the stage management team to familiarise themselves with the show.

Final run-throughs
Props call
Cue synopsis
Costume call

'Do you think that she's going to try and get all that on board?'

Final run-throughs

The company will begin to run the show from start to finish during the final week of rehearsals. This enables the performers to get a feel for the production as a whole, and to work on pace and timings. The director will require the deputy stage manager (DSM) to time each act, and as a result may decide to cut sections or pare down lines to make the production more accessible to an audience.

As the director and performers begin to finalise decisions about moves, actions, use of props and furniture etc the DSM can begin to finalise the setting and running plots. The stage manager (SM) can also begin to feed all the actual props into rehearsals for the runs. This enables the performers to become accustomed to the weight and shape of the actual props before the technical rehearsal.

Various designers and members of the production team will attend these run- throughs:

- The lighting designer needs to ascertain exactly which areas of the stage are used during the different scenes in order to finalise the LX plan.
- The set designer will ensure the performers have a good understanding of the layout of the staging.
- The costume designer and wardrobe supervisor will note the movements of the performers to ensure the costumes are going to enhance and not inhibit.
- Dressers may attend to get to know the show in detail to assist them with the costume changes.
- Lighting and sound operators also need to get a feel for the show.
- Front of House staff should see at least one run-through so they are well informed when advising the public about the production.
- The SM and ASM should attend as many run-throughs as time will allow. It is extremely helpful to them if the DSM has written up the setting and running plots by this stage. This allows the SM and ASM to assist in setting up for the runs and even get involved with any scene changes there may be. If the rest of the team get to know the show well before the technical rehearsal, it will save time and energy during the technical itself.

The SMgt team can also:

- Note where their tasks take place during the action of the production so that they are aware of how much time there is between cues.
- Note the movement of the props and, more importantly, where they end up! Some of the smaller props and personal props can be left in the strangest places so it is in your own interest to know these secret places. This information will save many frustrating minutes when setting back.
- Pre-empt potential problems, eg: doorway not wide enough to take a large prop or piece of furniture during a scene change.
- Spot if any performers are miming props and find out if the director wishes it to be included. Obviously, the DSM is watching out for this throughout the rehearsal period, but the more eagle eyes the better.

- Acquire a more intimate knowledge of the show and be better equipped to run the technical rehearsal more efficiently.
- Meet the performers again, which will assist in building a good working relationship. It is important that the SMgt team makes an effort to communicate with the performers. The DSM will have spent a few weeks in rehearsals with them, but the SM and ASM spend that time propping. The better you know your company the more sympathetic you are to their needs during the show.
- Enjoy the show from the front! Once the team move into the performance space, it is likely that their only view will be from one wing or the other.

Props call (props spread)

Many companies (though not all) will have a props call during pre-production week. It involves laying out all the props neatly on tables, usually scene by scene. The SM will read through the props list showing the director and designer each prop in turn. The DSM will liase with the director and SM in terms of confirming the position and practical usage of each item. The ASM will take notes of any cuts, additions or alterations to be made, while the SM ticks each item in the 'passed' column.

This is a very useful and beneficial part of the propping process for the following reasons:

- It allows the director and designer to double check all the props they have passed during the rehearsal process. If they passed a prop in week 1 of rehearsals, and haven't seen it since (often the case with very valuable or delicate borrows), then it may be that the prop

The props call

doesn't now fit with the rest of the piece. The blocking may have subtly changed, which could change the practical use of that item.

- It is reassuring for the designer, director and the SMgt team to check all props and furniture in this way before the technical rehearsal, to allow time for changes and alterations to be made.
- It is important visually for the director and designer to see all the props and furniture together to ensure a consistent style. They will also be able to ascertain if these items will fit with the colour and overall design concept contained within the set and costumes.

Cue synopsis

This session tends to be a bit of a luxury afforded to colleges and larger companies – those with more time available in pre-production week. The main objective is to go through all the cues in the show, deciding which effect goes where in relation to the script.

- The director leads this session by discussing with the rest of the team what effect they wish to create, where the cues come, and how long lighting and sound fades will be. Always in the correct order so the cues can be numbered.
- The lighting designer discusses each lighting cue with the director and agrees on each input point and the fade times.
- The sound designer discusses each sound effect, and agrees on the input point and fade times.
- The lighting and sound operators will attend to take relevant notes, and to get to know the cues and their intended effects.
- The production manager takes a note of every cue discussed and fills in the cue synopsis sheet. This is then distributed to the relevant Heads of Department. See template on page 142.

Example of cue synopsis sheet:

Cue Synopsis

Show: *The Picnic Hamper*   **Date:** 10-8-99

Page	Cue	Description	Input Point	Time up/down	Notes
I	LXI	Fade house lights	Front of house clearance	7 secs	
I	SQI	Fade pre-show music		7 secs	
I	CLI	Cue performers S.L.	On blackout (B/O)		
I	LX2	Fade up general	As performer start singing	5 secs	
I	SQ2	Bell chimes	'…where is he now?'	S.S.	
I	LX3	General X special C.R.	Follow on (F/O) from SQ2	5 secs	
I	Fly QI	Fly in wall	'…enough I say…'		
I	CL2	Cue performers C.R.	Once wall is on it's dead		
I	LX4	Fade up lamp special	As Gareth switches on light	Snap	Visual

- The DSM inserts the position of the cues, the order in which they come, and their relation to the script directly into the book. Any cue lights required to cue the performers on-stage will be inserted at this point. Note how the list of cues on the Cue synopsis sheet are translated into 'the book'. Also note the abbreviations one could use in the description column.

Example of prompt copy with input points:

Script	Instruction	Cue	Description	Blocking

	SB LX 1-4
	       SQ 1-2
	       CL 1-2
	       Fly Q1			

	FOH CL	LX1 – Go SQ1 – Go	H.L. + Preset 7" ♩ ↓ 7"	
	On B/O	CL1 – Go	Ⓖ+ⓈSL	
	As Ⓖ & Ⓢ sing	LX2 – Go	GEN. ↑ 5"	
		SQ2 – Go	CHIMES	
	F/O	LX3 – Go	GEN. ✗ SP 5"	
		FlyQ1 – Go	WALL ↓	
	Wall on dead…	CL2 – Go	Ⓜ+ⓉCR5"	
	Ⓐ switches light	LX4 – Go	LAMP ↑	
	CALL Ms Maclean Mr Wild			
	CURTAIN UP ACT 1			

Key to cue description abbreviations

H.L. – House lights	↑ – LX fade up	♩ – Music
GEN. – General LX state	↓ – LX fade down	S.P. – LX special
Ⓥ – Visual	< – sound fade up	5" – 5 seconds
✗ – Crossfade	> – sound fade down	5' – 5 minutes

If a company do not have the time for this session, the DSM is expected to glean the above information from rehearsals and from discussions with the director. The cue synopsis sheet will be distributed to the relevant departments before production week. The exact positions of the cues (input points) are then written into the book during the plotting session. There are several benefits of having a cue synopsis session before the technical rehearsal:

- It allows this particular team to discuss each cue without the pressures of the plotting session or the technical rehearsal.
- The LX and sound team has more detail to work with before plotting the show.
- The position of cans and cuelights backstage can be confirmed before the technical.

• The DSM can call the cues to themselves quietly during the last few run-throughs, thus becoming better prepared for the technical. If this is their first book they can even spend some time practising sequences on the prompt desk using the cuelights. At college a student built a practice cuelights box which the students train on during run-throughs.

Calls

The DSM can now insert the following calls into the book in preparation for the technical.

• Stand bys
• Performers' calls
• Curtain up, interval warnings, and post show calls
• Pre-show calls

Stand bys

Before each cueing sequence the DSM gives a 'stand by' via the intercom system verbally and on cuelights, to all the operators involved in the imminent cues. As the operators do not know the show as well as the DSM, they require alerting to the fact that particular cues are coming up. The operators will respond to the DSM by saying 'standing by' verbally and responding to the cuelights so the DSM knows they are ready to take the cue. The position of the stand by, and how many cues you clump together, is entirely dependent on the type of equipment being used (manual or computerised lighting boards or sound desks), and how much time there is between each sequence. Usually the stand by is put in around about half to three-quarters of a page before the cue. The stand-bys should be given in the same order as the cueing sequence.

Performers' calls during the show

As a courtesy the DSM will call the performers via the show relay system from their dressing room, or green room, to the backstage area to await their entrance. The DSM should work out how long it might take for the performer to get from the dressing room to the stage and insert the call in the book accordingly (many dressing rooms may be up a few flights of stairs, or the performer might be wearing a cumbersome costume, or be elderly or disabled). All factors should be considered. The word 'call' and the performers names will be inserted in the book, but should be said in full, and repeated so the performer is certain to hear it, for example: 'This is your call Ms Palmer, Ms Fraser, Mr Graham and Mr Offin. Ms Palmer, Ms Fraser, Mr Graham and Mr Offin your call please. Thank you.'

Curtain up; interval warning; post show

A call is given backstage via the show relay system to announce the curtain is up on each act, for example: 'Ladies and Gentlemen, the curtain is now up on Act 1. The curtain is now up, thank you.' A warning bell/call to FoH staff is given from the corner to alert them to the interval or end of the show. At the end of a performance a post show is given backstage to thank the company and give the call for the next performance, eg: 'Thank you very much ladies and gentlemen. The call for tomorrow is 6.55pm for a 7.30pm show. Thank you.'

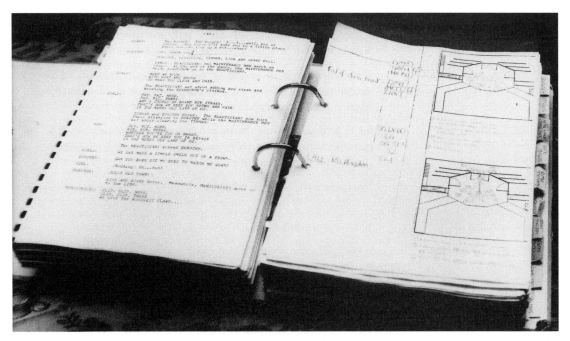

The prompt copy

Pre-show calls

All pre-show calls are timed around 'beginners' (which is 5 minutes before Curtain Up). The following calls assume the show goes up at 7.30pm.

The calls in bold refer to the calls given to Front of House (the audience); the rest to backstage (the performers). Calls are normally given by the DSM or SM.

6.55pm	Half hour	Good evening L+G, this is your half hour call, half an hour please, thank you.
7.10pm	Qtr hour	L+G this is your quarter of an hour call, 15 minutes please, thank you.
7.15pm	House open	**Good evening L+G and welcome to ... theatre. The house is now open for this evening's performance of... The house is now open, thank you.** L+G the house is now open. The house is now open, thank you.
7.20pm	Five minutes	L+G this is your 5 minute call. Five minutes please, thank you.
7.25pm	Beginners	L+G this is your Act 1 beginners call, Ms...., Mr...../Ms....., Mr...... your Act 1 beginners call. Thank you.

7.26pm	3 bells	**Good evening L+G and welcome to…Theatre. This evening's performance of…. will commence in 3 minutes, 3 minutes please L+G thank you.**
7.27pm	2 bells	**L+G will you please take your seats as this evening's performance will commence in 2 minutes, 2 minutes please L+G, thank you.**
7.28pm	1 bell	**L+G will you please take your seats as this evening's performance will commence in 1 minute, 1 minute please L+G, thank you.**
(7.30pm		FoH: clearance. Curtain up)
5 mins before curtain up Act 2		Act 2 beginners as above.
	3 bells	**L+G will you please take your seats. Act 2 will commence in 3 minutes, 3 minutes please L+G. Thank you.**
	2 + 1 bell	As above

Costume Call (costume parade)

The director, costume and set designers, wardrobe supervisor, production manager and, often, stage management will sit out front as each performer in turn parades their costume. Even though there will have been a number of fittings throughout the rehearsal period, this session affords the opportunity to examine each costume in detail in the presence of the full team.

- The director and designers are able to see a number of characters together who will be in the same scene to ensure a uniformity of style and colour.
- The performers have the chance to wear the costume before the technical rehearsal and comment on how well it fits and whether it feels correct for their character. They can also ensure it will be practical for the action required of their character.
- The wardrobe supervisor will take notes arising from the comments and suggestions made by the director, designers and performers. This allows the wardrobe department to make the necessary alterations before the technical rehearsal.
- The SMgt team can assist in making sure the costume call runs smoothly by ensuring the running order is adhered to, and calling the performers in turn so no time is wasted. If the SMgt team is involved in costume changes during the show (which incurs extra payment if on an Equity contract) they can become acquainted with the costumes and the wardrobe running plots.

Every department should now have collated all the necessary information in a recognisable and accessible format by way of accurate and detailed running and setting plots.

Each of these pre-production week activities (run-throughs, props call, cue synopsis and costume call) allow the team working the show to run an informed and smooth technical rehearsal. The team is now prepared to go into production week!

CHAPTER 6

PRODUCTION WEEK

'I hate long stand bys...'

Production schedule

Prior to the production week, the production manager will compile a detailed schedule of all work to be achieved during the production week. It should contain details concerning each department's tasks including timings for every activity. Many schedules will also state which members of the team and crew are called for what session and for how long. It is important that the layout and presentation of the schedule is such that it is visually accessible to the staff. Every schedule will vary enormously depending on the complexity of the show, and the number of people involved in the fit up. Production weeks are never long enough, so forward planning and interdepartmental co-operation is needed to accurately forecast timings for tasks.

The schedule will allocate time slots for:

- *The strike and get-out of the previous show*: dismantling and removing the set from the stage area.

- *Rigging LX*: the installation of lights following the lighting designer's plan.

- *Get in and fit up:* bringing in the new set and building it onstage.

- *Focusing:* focusing the lights to a pre-determined size and position onstage.

- *Plotting:* building each lighting state by bringing up lights individually to the desired level to compose a stage picture. This collection of levels is recorded manually or on a memory board, determining the timings to achieve fluidity from one state to another. Sound levels are also plotted individually.

- *Stage Management/Wardrobe setting up:* laying out all props, furniture, set dressing and costumes in their correct positions backstage and onstage.

- *The technical (the tech):* running through the show to ensure the cueing sequences, lighting and sound cues, costumes, props, furniture and scenery all work together in a cohesive way. At any point the director, SMgt team, designers or performers may call a hold to sort out any problems which may arise.

- *Dress rehearsals:* running through the show without stopping.

- *Previews:* public performances usually at a reduced rate to run the show in.

- *Opening/press night:* once the show has settled, and all problems have been ironed out the production is ready for the critics.

Example of a basic production week schedule:

Sat 8th	10.30pm	Strike/get out	3 x carpnters
		LX de-rig + rig onstage	3 x LX+1 x sound
Sun 9th	9.00am	Install rostra floor	3 x carpenters
		Fly ceiling piece	1 x Flyman
		Construct spiral staircase	
	1.30pm	Carpenters break	
		LX rig FoH	4 x LX
	2.30pm	Carpenters get in flats + erect	
		Hang blacks upstage	
	5.30pm	Tea break	
	6.30pm	Carpenters continue onstage	
	11.30pm	Paint call	2 x painters
Mon 10th	9.00am	SMgt mark furniture for focusing	
	9.30am	Focus (carpenters potter)	4 x LX
	1.00am	LX break (workers for carpenters)	2 x carpenters
	2.00pm	Continue focusing	
	6.00pm	LX tea break/carpenters finish off	
	7.00pm	LX plotting	
Tue 11th	9.00am	Continue LX plotting/sound plotting	
		SM set up/tidy backstage	
	11.30am	LX finish plotting/SM set up onstage	
		Scene change rehearsal	
	1.00pm	Lunch/Fire Officer visit	
	2.00pm	Risk assessment with cast/walk the set	
	2.30pm	Begin technical	
	6.00pm	Tea break	
	7.00pm	Continue technical	
	11.00pm	Break	
Wed 12th	10.00am	Continue technical	
	1.00pm	Lunch	
	2.00pm	Continue technical	
	5.30pm	Tea break/SM set back	
	6.55pm	Half hour call/checks	
	7.30pm	1st Dress rehearsal	
	10.30pm	Performers break/tech notes	
Thu 13th	9.00am	Tech work onstage/rehearsals as called	
	11.30am	SM set up	
	12.25pm	Lunch	
	1.25pm	Half-hour call/checks	
	2.00pm	2nd Dress rehearsal	
	5.00pm	Performers break/SM set back	
	6.55pm	Half-hour call/checks	
	7.30pm	1st Preview	
Fri 14th	7.30pm	2nd Preview	
Sat 15th	7.30pm	Press Night	

Order of events

The specific responsibilities of the SMgt team will vary depending on the size of the company. In large companies SMgt will not be involved with the rigging, fit up or even setting up the props, however in small scale companies the team may be involved in all the above activities. The model shown below represents many middle scale rep companies. The production manager will oversee, drive and may assist in each part of the process. It is their responsibility to ensure the schedule is adhered to and last minute spending does not create overspends. They also deal with all matters relating to Health and Safety.

Rigging

*   SMgt assist where necessary.

Fit up

*   SMgt assist where necessary.

Focusing

*   Before the focusing session SMgt mark the position of furniture (and may provide some of the actual furniture if it is not required in rehearsals).

Plotting/Setting up

*   During plotting the SM and ASM begin to clear the backstage area of all the fit up detritus and will lay all the actual props out on the backstage props tables. It is good practice to neatly lay out all the props on the props table, then section off each prop with masking tape in order to name every item. This ensures no items get missed during the props check, as it is easy to spot an empty area which indicates that prop has not yet been set *(see diagram on page 84)*.
*   Leave a space at one end of the props table for show running plots, and a space at the other end for props coming offstage.
*   Lay runners (strips of carpet or matting) down in any backstage areas where people will be walking to reduce noise from footfalls. This also indicates where it is safe to walk.
*   Check all cables are taped down.
*   Mark all edges of scenery and equipment with white tape to avoid tripping and bumps.
*   Note the backstage black spots and ask LX to rig sufficient working lights (usually low output with blue gel, or with blue bulbs inserted).
*   Check all fire extinguishers are in their correct positions. Mark their positions with white tape so that they remain in the same position throughout the run.
*   Remove any items that are not directly needed for the performance. i.e. boxes or stage weights ready to leap out and trip up an unsuspecting passer-by.
*   Sweep and vacuum all areas. It is very important to be diligent when clearing the backstage area in readiness for the company using it. There may be performers in bare feet or elaborate costumes, which could snag on stray nails or staples.

- If your backstage area is neat, props tables clearly marked and all edges marked with white tape you are providing a safe working environment for the company.
- The ASM(s) may be required to walk the lights (standing in for the performers to ensure the correct area and faces are lit). They may also assist the DSM to reset furniture for different scenes.
- Meanwhile, the DSM is sitting out front in the auditorium with the director and lighting designer as they plot the lighting states into the board. This is the point where the DSM will insert all the cues if they are not already in the book.

Post-plotting/pre-technical

- The SMgt team will require some time onstage once all the other departments have finished to sweep, vacuum, mop and set up all the remaining props and furniture. From this point onwards the setting up will be led by the stage manager. This session gives the DSM an opportunity to hand over responsibility and to clarify any queries the rest of the team may have with reference to the positions of items and their relation to the setting plot.

Props table

- If the show requires set dressing the designer and the SMgt team arrange the extra items where they will enhance the set without interfering with the action.
- If it is a big show, with complicated scene changes, then the team may have a scene change rehearsal or dry tech (session without performers).

Things they never said

Extracts from 'Flyman' *(The Stage and Television Today)*

The technical rehearsal

- It looks as though there'll be time for a third dress rehearsal
- Take your time setting back
- We've been ready for hours
- I can't hear the band
- That didn't last long

SM	Can we do that scene change again please?
LX designer	Bit more light from those big chaps at the side. Yes that's right, the ones on stalks whatever they are called.
Electrics	All the equipment works perfectly.
Musicians	So what if that's the end of a call. Let's just finish this bit off.
Wardrobe	Now, when exactly is the first dress rehearsal?
Workshop	I don't want anyone to know, but if you insist then yes, I admit it, I have just done an all-nighter.
Performer	This costume is so comfortable.

The technical rehearsal

At this point in the production week the SMgt team have a wider remit – that of company care. The full company will be called for the technical rehearsal. The team has to ensure that the performers know which dressing rooms they are in (names posted on dressing room doors) and be prepared to answer any queries the performers may have. It is essential that the team is ready to begin the tech on time, as they also have to ensure the well being of the performers.

Pre-show checks consist of:

- Ensuring all other departments have done their checks.
- Checking the whole company are signed in (on the sign-in sheet compiled by SMgt) and are in good health.
- On and offstage props and furniture checks. It is vital that two people do the checks each performance on- and offstage – one to read from the list, and/or diagram, and one to see the item and say 'check' or 'yes'. This ensures that no item is missed. Imagine you have been working on the same show for six weeks, two shows a day. I have been caught out, thinking I saw the item there, only to realise I saw it during the checks of the earlier show.
- Handing out personal props and collection of performers' valuable items by the DSM during the half. This also gives the DSM the opportunity to say hello to their company, and to answer any last minute questions.
- Tabs in / workers off / blues on.

- As mentioned in the previous chapter the DSM will also be giving all the pre-show calls from the prompt desk.
- If there are naked flames or pyrotechnics in the show the SM or PM will have contacted the local Fire Officer, or Building Control Officer, to discuss how each effect works. Before the technical can begin the Fire Officer should visit the set and be shown the position and effect in situ. If they are happy that the effects are safe, and that suitable precautions are being taken, then they will issue a form giving written permission to perform the effects.

Responsibilities during the tech:

- Before the tech begins the PM will call the full company onstage and go through the Risk Assessment with everyone. This involves talking and walking the performers round all areas of the set. Each point raised on the risk assessment form will be discussed in detail. The company will be advised of any hazards and how to avoid them or what precautions should be taken to make a potentially dangerous action safe. For example steep steps, offstage ramps, high acting areas, moving scenery etc (see Chapter 9).
- The PM may sit out front in the auditorium making technical notes as the tech proceeds, compiling a list of the jobs still to be finished off. In this way the PM can call various members of the production team during lunch and tea breaks, making the most of available onstage time. The role of the production manager varies from company to company. Some may take a much more active role than others during the tech. It is dependent on the way the director likes to work, the physical layout of the theatre and the particular strengths of the SMgt team.
- The SM will float from backstage to onstage. If it is a small team she will be actively involved in backstage activities and scene changes. In a larger team he will oversee all the activities of their team and stage crew and be free to troubleshoot as the need arises. If the action stops, or the SM feels the performers onstage need to stop, she will shout 'hold please'. The minute this call is given the SM must appear onstage to help sort out that particular problem. She will liaise with the DSM on a suitable pick-up line, and should be ready to resume as soon as possible.
- The DSM has a major role to play in a tech. In many theatres, the DSM sits out front if there is a prompt desk position in the auditorium. This enables effective communication between the director, the SMgt team and the performers. If they do not have this facility the DSM will be situated in the prompt corner or control room. They cue the operators, and call and prompt the performers. They may call 'hold' if there are cueing problems. The minute the action has stopped they should decide the best place from which to restart the action, and advise the performers of a suitable line. They will then instruct the operators to set back to a specific set of cues and wait until they are reset. Once set back the DSM says 'thank you' or similar to the performers so they know that the technical team is ready to begin again. The DSM's energy and forward thinking can help drive the tech forward.
- The ASM(s) assists the SM in all the backstage activities, as well as being responsible for their own specific tasks. Both the SM and ASM make detailed notes throughout the tech of all cuts and additions to either the setting of props or the running plots. Again I stress the need to be pro-active. For example, if an ASM sees a performer struggling off with an awkward prop they can assist by paging the masking or as a performer rushes offstage to do a costume change they drop a suitcase in the middle of a walkway an ASM can clear it to the props table.

All these small but significant tasks should be noted and later added to the master running plot. It is also beneficial to keep a very close eye on how the performers handle getting props from the props table. If necessary ask them if they wish that item set in a different place offstage to make its retrieval easier. This will then be altered on the setting plot.

It is of prime importance to facilitate the performers during the performance. They should feel confident that the SMgt team will execute all the tasks with the same diligence and consistency for each performance.

The SMgt team should:

- GIVE ATTENTION TO DETAIL
- BE PROACTIVE
- BE SUPPORTIVE AND CONSISTENT
- REACT POSITIVELY TO ALL REQUESTS

Post-tech/pre-dress

- After the tech there is usually a notes session with the SMgt team, designers, operators, the PM and director. This affords an opportunity to iron out any problems that were not addressed during the tech and to tighten up cueing sequences. The director and designer will also give notes on props and costumes that need altering. This allows informative and positive feedback encouraging the production team to keep working on perfecting the show. These sessions will happen after each dress rehearsal and on into the run for as long as there is a need to tighten up the show.
- Between the tech and the dress the SM and ASM will rewrite the running and setting plots. Once all the changes have been made to the plots the team can set back all the props and furniture. Check with the performers that they are happy with the setting of their props, and whether there is anything else they need assistance with during the show.
- The DSM should attend the notes session that the director has with the performers. There may be queries that the DSM can assist with, and which can then be passed on to the rest of the production team.

The Dress Rehearsal

The pre-show sequence, setting back, checks and the running of the show is similar to the tech. The main differences between the tech and the dress are:
- The backstage team and performers have the opportunity to run the show in real time. This may highlight major timing difficulties in costume or scene changes. Any problems can be discussed at the notes session after the dress and rectified before the second dress.
- The SMgt team can check that their setting and running plots work.
- The DSM will take accurate timings of each act and inform the director. They will also fill in a show report from the first dress and throughout the run, which is distributed to relevant Heads of Department *(see template, page 136)*.

The dress should not stop unless there are serious problems, or there is a safety risk.

The Show Report

The function of a show report is to inform the director, who may not be present at every performance, of any deviations from the script or cueing.

The DSM will make a note of any operational problems, inappropriate behaviour from the company, timings of each act, and audience numbers and response. The SM may add any comments they have noted from a backstage point of view and sign it.

Show Report

Show: *The Lizards*			No: 2
Signed: DSM & SM			Date: 14/1/00

Act / Interval	Up	Down	Time
Act 1	7.30pm	8.35pm	1 hr 05 mins
Interval	8.35pm	8.55pm	20 mins
Act 2	8.55pm	10.05pm	1 hr 10 mins

Total running time:	2 hrs 35 mins

Total playing time:	2 hrs 15 mins

Notes:

1. SQ34 was cued late as Mr Pritchard dropped the line: 'where's my bouffe?'
2. The golden gnome fell over in Scene 3. Will be fastened more securely.
3. Ms Steele knocked over the bottle of wine in Scene 4, but was covered well by Mr Storie.

Comments: The House was full. A warm and responsive audience. A tight show, with energetic pace.

Cc: Director, prompt copy, Designers, Workshop, Wardrobe.

Prompt desk

The Previews and First Night

Weeks of designing, building, rehearsing, propping and ultimately the long and arduous hours of production week culminate here. The finishing touches to the set, tweaking of lamps, re-writing of cues and plots are made, and the show is now ready for the audience.

Every company hope their production is received well, and due recognition given to the creative skills and efforts of the performers, design and production teams. There is nothing to match the adrenaline rush as the house lights fade or, equally, the feeling of relief and satisfaction when the curtain comes down to applause from an appreciative audience.

Layout of props table

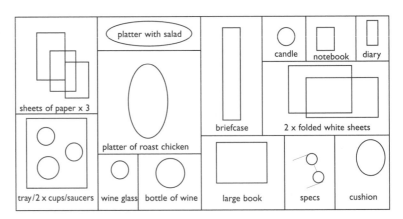

CHAPTER 7

THE RUN

'What do you mean, you couldn't find the marks so you've brought it back off?'

Now the show is up and running the SMgt team will:

* Clear the rehearsal room in preparation for the next set of rehearsals.
* Return rehearsal props and furniture to stock.
* Return any props that are not actually required in the show.
* Ensure all setting and running plots are legible and accurate.
* Send programmes off to all the businesses and individuals they have borrowed from with their credit underlined and a 'thank you for helping with this production' slip.
* Check all props are maintained, and buy any necessary comestibles.

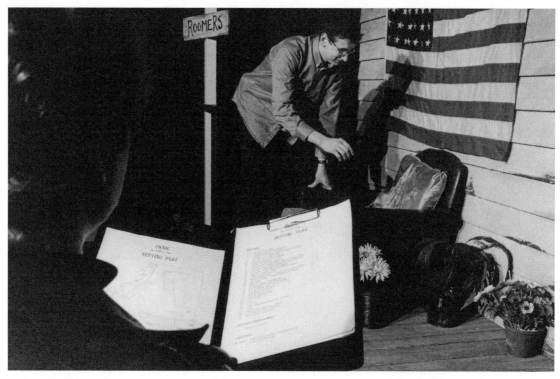

Pre-show checks

Things they never said

Extracts from 'Flyman' *(The Stage and Television Today)*

Admin	The level of overtime payments here are simply unacceptable. Our backstage staff deserve better.
Box Office	Comps? No problem.
Set designer	You're right, it looks dreadful.
Flyman	No, my lips are sealed. What I may or may not have seen remains a secret.
Electrics	That had nothing to do with the computer, it was my fault..
Crew	No, no, I'm sure that's our job.
SMgt	Thanks, but I don't drink.
Performer	Let me stand down here with my back to the audience.
Chippie	I can't really manage those big fast power tools myself. I prefer to use these little hand drills.
All	Let's go and ask the Production Manager. He'll know.

In Repertory theatre, where the team starts rehearsing and propping the next show almost immediately, the SMgt will follow a daily routine.

Morning	Prop and rehearse next show
Early afternoon	Prop and rehearse next show
Late afternoon	Set up for evening performance
Evening	Run the show

In large scale touring or commercial theatre the team may have regular understudy rehearsals to run, maintenance, ordering and paperwork to organise during the day. The evening consists of setting up, checks and running the show.

Crisis Management

During the run the health and well-being of the company, and the smooth operation of the show, are the responsibility of the SM.

- The SM should be made aware of any problems immediately, who will either deal with it or delegate to the relevant person.
- Each night check all performers are in good health. If one or more is not, then be prepared to deal with immediate problems as they arise.
- Know the fire drill and evacuation procedure.
- Know the position of all backstage fire extinguishers.
- If the show has to stop for whatever reason, bring in the tabs, fade up the Houselights, and make an announcement to the audience as soon as possible. An example might be 'Ladies and Gentlemen, due to unforeseen circumstances we are unable to continue this evening's performance. Would you please leave the auditorium by the nearest exit, as directed by our ushers. Thank you for your co-operation.'
- Be attentive to the action at all times and therefore ready to deal with any emergency calmly.
- Keep a basic tool kit, LX and gaffa tape and a torch close to the props table for running repairs.
- Make sure the First Aid Kit is stocked up and close at hand.
- In the event of an injury to a member of the company it is a legal requirement that an accident/incident report book or form is filled in by the SM. Copies should then be given to:

The injured party
Administration
The Health and Safety Officer
The prompt copy

This ensures that the event is recorded accurately and agreed by all parties in case of injury claims at a later date.

- One can never prepare for the numerous events that can and do happen. The Risk Assessment can alert the company to many of the potential hazards but staying alert and thinking ahead can assist with most eventualities.
- The intercom system (cans) which links all individuals working the show is an integral part of crisis management. For this reason certain guidelines should be followed. Never speak after 'standbys' have been given before a cueing sequence. Observe a respectful silence after 'beginners' as the DSM has to concentrate on the FoH calls, and always be aware that anyone could be listening in!
- Experience is a double-edged sword. The more productions one works on, the more problem solving one deals with. However, with that experience comes the widening knowledge base of all the things that can go wrong. As a long serving stage manager I look back fondly upon the early days of sweet naiveté!

One of the main aims of the performers and backstage team is to keep the production fresh. It is all too easy to slip into complacency. If this does happen it has far reaching effects, not just from an artistic point of view but from the Health and Safety angle also. The company must work together to maintain the standards set by the director during the production week. The show report can act as a method of informing the director of problems, which can prompt positive adjustments. Each individual, however, should endeavour to remain disciplined and true to the original intent of the piece.

It would be unfair to end this section on such a serious note. In conclusion I must add what an exhilarating and challenging experience running a show is. The camaraderie and teamwork, the amusing conversation over cans (during pages with no cues whatsoever) and those hysterical moments when something retrievable goes wrong....

1. One lead actor from a southern rep decided to start from the top again – 15 minutes into the action – because he had messed up the laying down of essential plot and props arrangement. He turned to the prompt corner (in front of an audience of approximately 800) and asked if all the props could be set back, and the show begun again. We dutifully ran around the stage (no tabs!) and re-set all the props including a very long fire-hose, which had to be rewound by taking it out into the auditorium and slowly coiled back onto the drum. It was a moment of total embarrassment for the SMgt team. The operators set back also, and we re-ran the opening sequence. The aforementioned actor re-appeared to rapturous applause. The audience had loved it.

2. A Scottish Rep had a line of actors standing to attention having just come out of a row of army shower cubicles, dressed in little white towels. A ripple of shoulder shaking begins onstage as the actor standing centre is aware of his little white towel beginning to unravel itself. The audience also becomes aware of the impending disaster, and the whole theatre erupts as the towel falls to the stage revealing all.

These are but a few of the many wonderful moments, and I'm sure anyone who is involved in theatre has their own collection of similar stories. What a book that would make!

The final performance and the strike

In preparation for the last night the PM will draw up a strike plan. After consultation with the rest of the production team, a schedule giving the order of the strike and who is called will be distributed to all relevant departments.

The SMgt team can prepare for the strike by sorting out boxes, skips and newspapers for quick packing. During the show the team will remove any props and furniture which are not needed again.

The strike

- The PM is responsible for the safe removal of all scenery, lighting and sound equipment, furniture and props from the stage area. They oversee the whole operation and assist and motivate where necessary.
- The SMgt team should strike all the props and furniture as quickly as possible to the backstage areas in order to allow the rest of the crew to begin the set strike.
- The DSM will collect all the personals before the performers leave and the costumes struck from the dressing rooms. All too often the smaller items can disappear at this point, so it is imperative that the DSM gets round as quickly as possible to rescue any props that could get lost in a costume or leave with a forgetful performer. Occasionally a performer may become particularly attached to a prop, and wish to keep it as a momento. The DSM tidies the prompt desk, removing all cards, good luck charms and tape indicating cuelights. It is also good practice to clean away the sweetie papers etc from inside the desk leaving it presentable for the next DSM. They then collect all the running plots from SMgt, lighting, sound, wardrobe, flyman and crew to store in the prompt copy.
- The SM and ASM(s) continue to remove all items from the backstage area to their relevant boxes or storage to await returns. If possible any props and furniture from stock should be replaced in the props and furniture store that night. All runners are lifted and returned to storage. In smaller companies the team can then join the crew onstage to assist with the rest of the strike and ensure the theatre is swept and tidy before leaving.

Returns

On the next working day after the strike all borrowed or hired items should be returned, and all paperwork submitted to the production file.

- It is worth the extra effort to check over each prop or piece of furniture thoroughly for any signs of damage. There are many products on the market that are excellent for smoothing over tiny scratches in wood (although I have found a mix of linseed oil and turps is cheap and effective). If you are returning silver, bronze, copper, glass or crockery items give them a quick clean or polish. It is essential to return the items in pristine condition in order to further good relations with the companies and individuals you have cultivated.
- If there are items which have been broken or severely damaged be prepared to offer suitable compensation. Some companies are very understanding and may waiver the cost, but one cannot be presumptive.
- If for whatever reason it is not possible to return a prop on the agreed date then phone to arrange another suitable time. Many antique shops rely on the items being returned

promptly in order to get them back on the shelves to sell, and may get anxious if there is a delay with no explanation.

- On returning props and furniture take your copy of the borrow form with you to get signed. Also ensure they sign their top copy so they have their own record of the item(s) being safely returned.
- Be as pleasant on returning as you were when you collected the items. It is always a rush to get everything back in one or at the most two days, but it is important to take the time to have a chat about how the production went and show your gratitude for their assistance.
- On returning to base tick off the master borrow book and return all the signed borrow forms to the production file.

Example of master borrow book completed:

Date	Item	Contact	Initials	Comp	Credit	Borrow/ Hire/ Donation	Actual Rt date	By whom
8/9/99	4 x wine goblets 4 x knives 4 x forks 4 x spoons 4 x napkins Tablecloth	Hospitality Manager, Goodyear Hotel, Old Road, Edinburgh. Tel 114-9876	GP	x 2	Done	Borrow	8/10/99	GP
9/9/99	Ream of parchment	Stationers, New Road, Edinburgh. Tel 123-1234	CC	x 2	Done	Donation	n/a	n/a
10/9/99	Pine dresser	Gibble Antiques, Ye Old Lane, Edinburgh.	TC	n/a	n/a	Hire	9/10/99	TC
10/9/99	Old bicycle	Pedals, Spoke Lane, Edinburgh.	NLW	x 2	Done	Borrow	9/10/99	TC
12/9/99	1940s radio	Mr Kindly, c/o Collectors Club. Tel 221-3456	GJB	x 2	Done	Borrow	12/10/99	GP

CHAPTER 8

MANAGEMENT TECHNIQUES

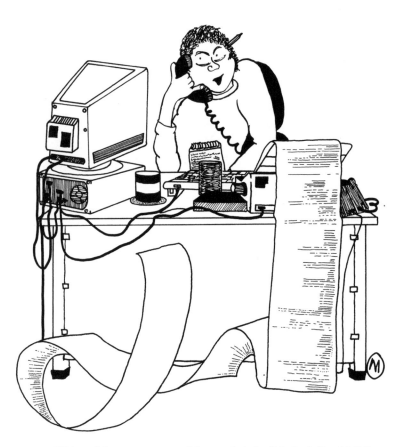

'I'll be with you as soon as I have printed off today's 'to do' list'

In previous chapters I have dealt with various methods that are used to achieve an efficient production process. But that is only half the picture. Basic stage management skills can be learnt easily and deployed effectively using common sense and initiative. The creative part of the job is to combine these methods with good management and communication skills. These topics form the mainstay of the role of stage management. Without a deep understanding of management techniques and the ability to communicate effectively the stage manager is just paying lip service to their responsibilities. This area underpins all SMgt work.

It would be foolish to attempt to re-write all the wonderfully illuminating books that already exist, so instead I will give an introduction to the subject and refer the reader to the book list found under 'Further reading' (page 133).

Systems management

This means using all your available resources as effectively as possible:

- Time scheduled effectively
- Money budgeted wisely
- Equipment handled safely
- Space used to its greatest advantage
- Efficient use of information technology

Managing yourself

Self organisation

- Master self-management before attempting to manage others.
- Decide what needs to be achieved then set about planning it.
- Don't fall into the trap of running around with pieces of paper looking busy without actually achieving anything.

Space management:

- Tidy your desk at the end of the working day in order to come to it clear the next day.
- Consider your work area: does it encourage order? The benefit of order is being able to find things quickly and save time, rather than waste time looking for important documents.

Points of order on the desk or in the office:

- Wall planner updated regularly.
- Display rehearsal notes.
- Display master props list.
- Display credits list.
- Display production schedule.
- Current phone books/contacts book near phone.
- All production paperwork filed in accessible format.
- Templates on disk filed appropriately.
- Reference books/research material easily accessible.
- Clear work areas encourage productivity.
- Encourage recycling policy for scrap paper.

Points of order in the props store:

- Keep it tidy where possible.
- Categorise all items into different areas.
- Ensure every item can be seen easily. This will save time when searching for specific props.
- On returning props, put back neatly in correct place.

Points of order in the furniture store:

- Ensure every item can be seen easily.
- Allow a walkway round store so furniture is accessible and can be removed easily.
- Compile a catalogue with photos and dimensions of all furniture to enable directors and designers to choose items without having to go to the furniture store (some theatres have the catalogue on disk so information and photos can be e-mailed).

Managing time

Possible diary format (see opposite):
- Time is an expensive commodity, so take time to plan.
- When planning time, be realistic. If you are asked how long a task will take do not under-estimate just to please. It will inevitably take longer than you think. Before embarking on any task try to work out how long it might take. After the task is completed compare the guestimate with the actual time taken. This will assist time planning the next time you do a similar job.
- Be in control of time – don't let it control you.
- Don't dither – learn to decide quickly what needs attention.
- Use a diary to ensure all meetings and calls are attended to and always be five minutes early for any meeting (allow for travel time).
- Sit quietly at the beginning of the day and work out what tasks must be achieved and then again at the end of the day reflect on tasks achieved. Empty your mind of all tasks to be achieved the next day into your diary or 'to do list'. In this way you will leave work with a clear head and the next day will be more organised.

'To do' list

- Prioritise your list. Always begin with the tasks that may be perceived as the most difficult or the most time consuming, or simply what must be done first.
- Put time aside to blitz the smaller, less important tasks on a daily basis. These jobs can clutter the desk, the 'to do' list itself and the mind. One method of dealing with this is: 'Do, Delegate, Ditch, but Decide.'
- Write down every task to be achieved and never rely on memory.
- In the early stages of propping, the props list will be the 'to do' list.
- As the list is realised it is pertinent to make up a more detailed list of specific tasks which may be split into different headings.

10.00	SMgt meeting (delegate tasks).
10.30	Meet props maker to discuss makes
11.00	Phone – NL to order fire retardant / Fire Officer
11.30	Phone re: borrows (desk, chairs, lamp, vase)
12.00	Production meeting
12.30	
1.00	Lunch
1.30	(1.45) Meeting with Director to update props list
2.00	Armchair upholstery
2.30	
3.00	
3.30	Collect – barrow, spades, fork etc from Fermers UK
4.00	
4.30	
5.00	SMgt debrief
5.30	Tea
6.00	
6.30	
7.00	Set up and checks
7.30	
8.00	Performance 12
8.30	
9.00	
9.30	
10.00	Break

For example:

During a production week the 'to do' list will comprise notes of minor adjustments to be made to the props and furniture. For example:

- The knitting should be six inches longer
- Braiding on armchair to be green
- Break down the plant pot
- Find another cup and saucer
- Documents to be opened as part of the action
- Break down carpet bag

Example of a 'To do' list

Makes	To buy
Carpet bag	Material for chairs
4 x letters	Parchment paper
Flower centrepiece	Silk flowers
Confetti	
Knitting	
Embroidery	
Pick Ups	**To get passed**
6 x chairs	Canes
Set of crockery	Wicker basket
Milk churn	Handkerchiefs
	Cigar box

Questions

When does the director want actual crockery in rehearsals?
What time is the run on Thursday?
Can the Gladstone bag be black rather than brown?

Staying healthy

Good food

To help maintain the high energy levels required in the theatre profession, it is wise to develop an informed and sensible attitude to what we eat and drink. The body requires a balanced diet of protein, carbohydrates, fat, vitamins, minerals and fibre to sustain health and energy.

The demanding hours and shortage of meal breaks can often lead to a general deficiency in many of the nutritional requirements mentioned above. Eating a little of the right foods often can keep the body going during very busy periods.

There are hundreds of books on the market which give good advice on what a balanced diet consists of, and many have suggestions and recipes for people with a busy lifestyle. You are what you eat, as they say, and it's worth making the effort!

Good health

We all fall prey to infections, viruses, minor illnesses and injuries from time to time. Most of us have an area of weakness, so when we are run down the same problem can come back time after time. Your first port of call should be your GP but if you find conventional medicine isn't helping, or you have to keep taking the same medication for long periods of time perhaps you need to take a hard look at the deeper reasons for chronic (long-term) conditions.
Many conventional medications just treat the symptoms, whereas there are many and varied types of complimentary medicine that work on the underlying weaknesses. Of course, one should consult a qualified practitioner for these therapies.

- *Homeopathy* A natural healing process in which remedies help the patient regain health by stimulating the natural healing energy of the body. The principles work on treating 'like with like' but in vastly diluted quantities. They are safe, non-toxic, and non-addictive.
- *Herbalism* Herbs have played a vital role in healing for over 4500 years. In Chinese herbal medicine illness is regarded as a sign of an imbalance within the whole person, and herbs are used to restore the balance. In this way the body's natural healing mechanisms are stimulated into working more effectively.
- *Acupuncture/Shiatsu/Reflexology* Like the ancient Chinese art of acupuncture, shiatsu and reflexology work on the flow of energy that circulates through the body in specific channels. By steadying and re-balancing this energy flow, health is improved and many illnesses alleviated. Acupuncture uses small needles to stimulate the pressure points, whereas shiatsu and reflexology use finger and hand pressures on the body or feet respectively.
- *Remedial massage* Excellent for treating pain and tension of the soft tissue (muscles, ligaments and tendons). Can also assist with stimulating the circulatory, digestive and lymphatic system.
- *Osteopathy* Re-alignment of the spine may assist with many long-term muscular and postural problems.

Stress management

A certain amount of stress can be beneficial to an individual, but it is important to recognise when too much stress begins to affect our health and effectiveness at work. Warning signs may include:

- Recurring or chronic illness
- A change in social/dietary habits
- Insomnia
- General feeling of fatigue
- A rise in consumption of cigarettes, alcohol or 'feel good' edibles
- An inability to effectively balance home and work demands
- Erratic mood swings
- A general decline in efficiency at work
- An inability to concentrate

Although it is impossible to attain a stress-free life, some of the following methods may help to reduce stress:

- *Exercise* Any physical activity will assist in reducing tension, stimulate circulation and help eliminate toxins from the body. Try to find some form of activity you can do easily, and fit into your lifestyle. For example: swimming, dancing, walking, cycling, gardening, sport, gym training etc.
- *Spoil yourself and be spoiled* Indulge yourself every now and then in a treat of some sort, such as a meal out, a new item of clothing, a long hot bath with a glass of wine etc. Also allow friends to spoil you.
- *Socialising* It's good to spend time with close friends and relax in good company. Try to talk openly about problems; a problem shared is a problem halved.

- *Pastimes/hobbies* Make time to do things that relax you, such as reading, listening to music, watching TV, going to the cinema etc.
- *Deep breathing* If you are in a particularly stressful situation it is helpful to take a few (two or three) deep breaths. Take the breath right down to the abdomen then release the breath slowly as you breath out. Think of the 'in' breath as refreshing and calming and the 'out' breath as eliminating the tension and toxins. Yoga and meditation teach this method in much greater detail and are both highly beneficial to stress relief.
- *Massage* Stress can manifest itself as headaches and tension in the neck and shoulders. Massage is extremely effective at relaxing the muscles around this area (or indeed any area that is tense and sore). It is very easy to learn the basics of massage from a practical guide. Once the basic strokes have been mastered, and you have practised on others, you can then ask for the favour to be returned. Alternatively, a qualified remedial masseur can treat you at a very reasonable cost (many theatres will have one who visits regularly).

Physical conditioning

In order to survive the very physical world of Stage Management it is essential to look after our muscles and keep them toned and healthy.

- Before doing any sort of physical work (fit ups, lifting/carrying furniture and scene changes etc) it is vital to ensure the muscles are warm and stretched. If the muscles are cold and tight it is very easy to damage the soft tissue.
- If possible try to do a little stretching first thing in the morning then more before any physical work.

Managing others

Team building

Whether you inherit or are building a team it is paramount to have a dynamic mix of personalities with varied skills. Much research has been undertaken into personality types and how they interact within a team. The following are two examples of different methods to analyse and evaluate the qualities an individual can bring into a team.

Dr. Meredith Belbin believed that each team member plays a dual role. Their main function being that of a manager, supervisor, deputy etc; then there is their *team* role. This role signifies what each person contributes to the process, as opposed to the content of the work. In identifying the individual's 'team' role we may balance the team as a whole. Belbin describes eight team roles, each member having a primary and secondary, or support, role.

1. The co-ordinator: organises and controls the activities of the team, using resources efficiently and effectively.
2. The shaper: gives shape or form to the team's activities.
3. The plant: generates the ideas and strategies.

4. The evaluator: analyses and evaluates the ideas and suggestions in terms of practicalities and feasibility.
5. The implementer: generates an action plan to implement the ideas and concepts.
6. The team worker: assists each individual in achieving and maintaining effectiveness.
7. The resource investigator: explores and develops outside resources and contacts.
8. The finisher: ensures nothing is overlooked and all loose ends are tidied up.

Carl Jung pioneered the study of personality types at the beginning of the century, He believed that we process and receive data via four main functions; thought, feel, sense and intuition. Each individual will have a leaning towards one or two of these types.

1. The thinker: enjoys tackling problems with logic and is good with facts, figures, accounting and finance.
2. The feeler: generates good team relations and has a perceptive, warm and sympathetic nature.
3. The sensor: strong on negotiation and troubleshooting and is practical and organised.
4. The intuitive person: has a strong imaginative sense and enjoys playing with theories and ideas.

These methods are outlined to highlight how unique each team member is, and how we may use this insight creatively in developing a more effective team.

A successful manager should:

- Be fair
- Communicate clearly and openly
- Be honest, decisive and direct
- Encourage an atmosphere of trust
- Be supportive
- Encourage new ideas
- Give and take constructive criticism
- Reward where relevant
- Show a high level of integrity
- Be trustworthy and reliable

Within a successful team, each individual should:

- Address every problem as a challenge
- Encourage high standards
- Encourage a good team spirit
- Be able to give and take constructive criticism positively
- Maintain a sense of humour
- Be as flexible and motivated as possible
- Be encouraged to contribute to decision making
- Develop a high standard of organisation
- Maintain respect for others
- Share a common goal with the rest of the team

Although these qualities have been split into managers and team members, most of these attributes are interchangeable. Many of the above skills can be built on successfully if the individual is taught how to recognise and evaluate their qualities. It is prudent for a manager to set objectives for the team and individuals, and to give regular feedback and appraisals at convenient intervals. This also allows the team members to provide feedback for the manager.

Delegation

It is paramount, when organising a team, to delegate effectively. Delegation is giving others responsibility and authority while you retain accountability and ultimate control; it is not to be confused with abdication. Try to foster the attitude that you are giving people the opportunity to achieve and develop, rather than just handing out jobs to be done.

Once you have assembled the team you can either allocate tasks, or ask the team to choose which tasks they would prefer to tackle. When delegating, the following process will ensure that the manager retains an overview of allocated work.

- Decide which tasks to delegate. The good manager will trust the team with most tasks, thereby freeing him or herself up to concentrate on pre-planning and departmental organisation.
- Decide upon the most relevant person to whom each task can be delegated. Determine the main strengths of each individual and allocate work accordingly. It may be pertinent to train up an individual in order to build on the overall team's abilities.
- Brief the delegates fully. Give details of deadlines, resources, and explain the desired outcome. Ensure each member has the full picture.
- Monitor progress from a distance, allowing the team to proceed free from interference. Encourage regular feedback. It is better if your team keep you up to date on their progress rather than having to chase after people. Maintain checks and balances to allow you to salvage things early when or if they go awry.
- Review achievements and give credit where credit is due.

Communication skills

To communicate effectively is to pass on all information as quickly and accurately as possible with the least amount of negative interaction. To achieve this requires well-developed skills in interpersonal techniques. Research has been carried out that suggests communication is 7% through words; 38% through tone; 55% through body language. These figures highlight the need to develop an awareness of the way we use tone and facial/body language in our professional communications. Here are some of the more obvious examples:

Positive tonal qualities:
- Interested
- Varied
- Lively
- Sympathetic

Positive body language   *Negative body language*

Negative tonal qualities:
- Aggressive
- Bored
- Sarcastic
- Whining

Positive body language:
- Arms open and relaxed
- Leaning forward
- Open expression
- Maintaining eye contact

Negative body language:
- Arms crossed
- Leaning back
- Closed, blank expression
- Looking down

Before any communication take a few seconds to ask yourself the following questions:

*   What is the main purpose?
*   What do I wish to achieve given the audience?
*   What is the best tone to use?
*   How much information do I need to give to be effective?
*   Is this the best time to communicate this information?
*   What type of communication will be most efficient?

There are three main ways to communicate a message:

1. *Memo/e-mail*
*   Enables you to reach many people simultaneously.
*   Allows the reader time to assimilate the information.
*   Personal contact is avoided.
*   Shows you have taken action.

2. *Telephone/net meeting*
*   Access to instant feedback.
*   Voice mail can pick up messages, allowing time to think about a response.
*   Allows you to assess the response to a certain extent.
*   Is more time efficient than person to person.

3. *Person to person*
*   Access to instant feedback.
*   Allows you to gauge the response immediately.
*   Gives the opportunity to generate a positive response.
*   Can convey message to many people simultaneously.
*   Allows for correction if misunderstood.

When using any of the above media:

*   Keep your message short and to the point.
*   Do not use jargon at all unless you can guarantee that it is shared.

Assertiveness

Assertiveness is being able to express one's own beliefs and opinions and to stand up for one's rights, while still respecting the rights, beliefs and opinions of others.

In order to communicate in a friendly, open and constructive way we should try to combine positive body language, tone and attitude. In negotiation it is important to try to achieve a win-win situation, in which both parties feel they have been successful. In all discussions using positive assertion will assist in accomplishing the objective.

We can identify three key positions:

- Unassertive: displays an inability to express an opinion, apologetic, hesitant and prefers giving in rather than standing up for their rights. This person may be regarded as weak and easily manipulated.

- Assertive: communicates in a confident, firm tone taking the other person's feelings into consideration while maintaining their own integrity. This person will gain respect and achieve more in life.
- Aggressive: communicates in a loud, abusive way threatening the rights and feelings of others and must win regardless. This person may get his own way, but will be disliked. This style could possibly encourage others to react in an aggressive way.

Consider, as an example, the following scenario, where person A wishes to borrow a tool from person B.

An unassertive response would be: 'Em... well I've only just bought it... but... I guess if you promise not to loose it... I might need it tomorrow... as long as I get it back... Ok then.'

An assertive response would be: 'I'm sorry, but it's new and I will be using it regularly so I would rather not lend it.'

An aggressive response would be: 'What would I want to do that for? No way, go buy your own!'

The assertive response ensures both parties' rights are observed. Obviously it is to everyone's benefit to be assertive in all communications. Such behaviour allows us to:

- Refuse unreasonable requests.
- Protect our personal rights.
- Respect the rights of others.
- Avoid unnecessary conflict.
- Openly discuss any issue.

Assertiveness training

It is possible to build on our assertiveness skills by raising our self-esteem. Consider the following points:

- Develop a better self-awareness: think about how you communicate with others, how they respond to you, and your ability to share your feelings. Ask friends for constructive criticism.
- Learn to express yourself: take chances occasionally and put forward your point of view when you might otherwise stay silent. You may be surprised at the positive response. Taking small risks every day can also help build confidence.
- Look after yourself: take care of your own health and well being through a good diet, exercise, sufficient sleep and relaxation. If you look after yourself you will feel better inside and out and will have a more positive attitude towards others and yourself.

Listening skills

Just as clear, direct and assertive discourse encourages good communication, so does the ability to listen effectively. How often do we leave a briefing or conversation not entirely sure of what was said, or expected of us? Or indeed felt that what we were trying to communicate was not picked up on correctly or accurately? In order to assist the speaker in communication, and ensure all information is assimilated correctly we need to develop good listening skills. During social interactions the functions of effective listening serve to:

- Give access to accurate information.
- Assist in focusing on the relevant points of the discussion.
- Convey an interest in the subject and speaker.
- Show concern and understanding.

To do this we practise 'active listening'.

Positive verbal signals:

- Feeding back the salient points.
- Giving encouraging noises, such as 'yes', 'I see' etc.
- Asking relevant questions.
- Giving positive responses at regular intervals.

Positive body signals

Negative verbal signals:

- Interrupting at inappropriate moments.
- Being argumentative and nit-picking.
- Muttering under breath.
- Sighing.

Positive body signals:

- Open and interested facial expressions.
- Sitting forward.
- Smiling, nodding etc.
- Maintaining eye contact.

Negative body signals:

- Bored or sleepy facial expressions.
- Slumped posture and folded arms.
- Fiddling with hair, pen etc.
- Avoiding eye contact.

Negative body signals

Barriers to effective listening

There are many situations where external and internal influences may be a hindrance to effective listening.

- Noisy, cold or uncomfortable environment.
- The subject matter is boring or irrelevant.
- Either party is unwell or depressed.
- A dislike for the speaker.
- Thinking of what to say next rather than listening carefully.
- One's mind is preoccupied.
- Lack of time.

In order to remember specific points or a set of given tasks it will be necessary to take copious notes. However if the discussion takes the form of a brainstorming or problem solving session, or is at all sensitive, then note taking may hinder the speaker and the listener's ability to respond appropriately. Work on the principle of 'need to know' and take notes afterwards if necessary while the memory is still fresh.

The creative art of stage management

Creative leadership

A manager will utilise and build on each individual's strengths, and manage the weaknesses. It is a creative skill to recognise and draw on the members' less obvious strengths and strive to harmonise the team.

Creative problem solving

The creative individual will learn how to approach a problem from a lateral perspective. The team may discuss the restraints (usually time and money) and focus on all the alternatives and various methods of solving the task. Through this brainstorming technique the team's ideas and creativity will as often as not come up with the solution. A good manager will listen to all ideas, give them ample consideration, evaluate, and then give suitable feedback. In allowing the team to take creative risks the team's overall problem solving abilities will improve and eventually benefit the whole team.

Creative scheduling

Creating a schedule involves the ability to take a set of activities to be achieved and fit them into the time allocated with a certain number of people. A schedule may be the production schedule created by the production manager or the daily and weekly time management lists the stage manager (or other heads of department) produces. In each case it requires creative juggling of all relevant factors and judicial scheming and lateral thinking to dovetail and overlap activities in the most effective and efficient way.

Creative budgeting

As with scheduling, a manager will juggle the given requirements of a production with the money available. The production manager is closely involved with the design process and will advise throughout what is financially possible and what is not. When faced with the entreaty: 'but we have to have this,' the production manager will use her creative skills to find an alternative way of providing what is required. During the build and production period money will often have to be cleverly reallocated between departments to provide the financial backup to the director and designer's demands.

Creative communication

A good stage manager will provide the production team with an effective method of communication. This needs very careful and considered use of communication skills to bring out the best in all team members. In this way a creative and empathic attitude is needed to deal with potential conflict of personal or production interests. All efforts should be made to encourage openness and trust. The deputy stage manager in rehearsals should handle the director and performers with a gentle but assertive attitude that is both supportive and, some might say, manipulative. The prudent deputy stage manager will anticipate the needs of the rehearsal process and create an organised and sympathetic environment to assist with the ongoing development of the production.

Creative propping

There is a huge difference between providing a collection of props and furniture which 'will do' and an accurate and beautiful array of items which sit comfortably within the piece. The main difference is in the background research and attention to detail the creative stage manager will provide. It is essential to absorb the concepts of the director and designer and research all items, even down to the design on a matchbox. When out propping one may be faced with a few choices for a particular item. If the stage or assistant stage manager has connected with the piece their creative ability will assist in picking the item which is 'just right'. This will not only give a period piece absolute authenticity but enable the performers to believe in their environment and allow the characters to grow even further once they begin to work on the set.

Creative cueing

During performance the DSM on the book has a very active role in contributing to the creativity of performance. They are like the conductor of an orchestra, dictating the pace of cueing sequences and blending the changes with the flow of the action. As with the performers, the deputy stage manager should instinctively feel when they have connected with the performance and become one with the creative energy which is the essence of live theatre.

CHAPTER 9

HEALTH AND SAFETY

'OK, stand by to open the green room fridge door...'

On entering employment it is necessary to know what the responsibilities of your employers are, and what you as the employee need to know.

Employers' responsibilities

Any organisation with more than five employees should have a Health and Safety policy. This policy provides details of the company's commitment to upholding the legal requirements and the resulting arrangements.

The Health and Safety at Work Act 1974 (HSWA) requires that 'safe systems of work be devised and implemented; that a safe place of work be provided and that plant and equipment is also safe and without risk to health and safety so far as is reasonably practicable'.
The Management of Health and Safety at Work Regulations 1992 (MHSW) require that written 'risk assessments' are undertaken for all work practices.

As a new employee one should expect an induction within the first week providing information on:

*   The organisation's Health and Safety policy.
*   The building's layout.
*   Fire and bomb alert evacuation procedures.
*   First aid facilities.
*   Training opportunities within the company.
*   Health and safety complaints procedures.
*   Accident report procedures.

Employees' responsibilities

The employee has a responsibility to him or herself, other employees, and the company to read the policy, understand its contents and to adhere to the safe working practices laid out in the document. It is also necessary to use common sense at all times and, if in doubt or tackling a new situation, to ensure suitable training has been provided.

In this way both employers and employees develop safe working practices and good management, which in turn not only prevents accidents but should cut down on time lost through injury and illness, increasing overall efficiency.

Health and safety applied to the production process

By its very nature the theatre environment can be full of potentially dangerous equipment, materials and situations. In the past all theatre practitioners have been aware of these hazards, identifying risks and dealing with them as part of the process. However, since 1992 it has been a legal requirement to make a formal notification of all potential hazards and their risk factors.

All issues concerning health and safety should be approached by identifying the risk involved and then assessing it. In any new situation (be it a new material, new piece of equipment or potentially hazardous activity) one should follow the process of doing a risk assessment then training where necessary.

The production manager may write a health and safety clause into the designer's contract then, once the design is realised, the model will also be assessed for potential risks.

During the build and rehearsal period the production manager will liase with the workshop and company to ensure all efforts are made to use safe working practices. He also has overall responsibility for overseeing a safe and controlled fit up period. Once the set is onstage the production manager may walk round the set with the equity deputy, then the performers, so that risks can be identified and the necessary precautions taken to ensure a safe environment. It is then the responsibility of the team and the performers working the show to adhere to the agreed safe usage of the space.

Examples of some potential hazards:

- Machinery: exposed moving parts should be guarded and only trained personnel permitted to operate them.
- Chemical substances: the appropriate working conditions must be observed as laid out in the COSHH regulations.
- Ladders, tallescopes etc: regular inspections carried out, and training given as to their safe use.
- Special effects, naked flames etc: all materials used in the set, props, furniture and costumes should be fire resistant or fire proofed. The local fire officer will inspect the set and issue a certificate of approval if all safe practices are observed.
- Lifting/carrying weights: precautions (eg: mechanical aids) and training given where there is a need to handle heavy equipment.
- Fire/ bomb alerts: all escape routes to be kept clear and all company members to be trained in fire evacuation procedures.
- Low light levels: gangways and hazards to be clearly marked in areas with low light levels.
- Over familiarity with potential hazards.

Please note this list is by no means exhaustive, and merely demonstrates a few of the areas that need to be considered in a production environment. The production manager will ensure that each department has completed a risk assessment for their area, materials and practices, and may have several different types of risk assessment forms to cover all eventualities.

Risk assessment

A risk assessment should:

1. Identify the hazard, and groups of people at risk (crew, public, cast etc).
2. State the type of injury/illness that may be sustained.
3. Estimate the risk factor (RF) involved before precautions are taken (by multiplying the severity of illness or injury by the likelihood of such an event occurring).
4. State what actions should be taken to reduce the risk.
5. Calculate the risk factor (RF) after precautions are taken.

Example of one type of production risk assessment form (see template on page 137):

Production Risk Assessment

Production: *The Deadly Deed*   Date: 27/2/99

Production Manager: Tash Walsh

Hazard	Potential loss	Risk factor before	Precautions	Risk factor after
Lifting sofa in scene change (SMgt)	Soft tissue injury / bruising	12	Manual handling training; protective footwear and gloves; use trolley	6
Low light levels backstage (Performers & SMgt)	Bumping, tripping, falling	16	White tape edges; lay runners over cables; provide blues where possible; use Maglight; keep all areas tidy	4
Sword fight (Performers)	Cuts, stab wounds, bruising	20	Use qualified choreographer; blunt points and blades; keep stage clear; rehearse and warm-up; non-slip flooring; check swords regularly	6
Use of naked flames (candles and cigarettes) (Full Company & Audience)	Igniting costumes, props, drapes. Hot wax spilling and burning	16	Ashtrays with sand and water; SMgt stand by with extinguishers; all items fireproofed; self-extinguishing lighters; consult Fire Officer	6

1-7 Low priority (acceptable risk)	8-14 Priority (requires attention)	15-25 High priority (unacceptable risk)

Calculating the Risk Factor

Severity	x	*Likelihood*
5 – Death / multiple casualties		5 – Inevitable
4 – Severe injuries		4 – Likely
3 – Serious injuries / time lost in excess 3 days		3 – Quite possible
2 – First Aid required / no time lost		2 – Unlikely
1 – No visible effects		1 – Improbable except in freak circumstances

Licensing

A venue

Theatres, cinemas and places of entertainment require a licence to confirm that the venue meets an acceptable level of safety. The local council office will issue one of two licenses:

1. A public entertainment licence, which covers music, concerts, cabaret and variety shows.
2. A theatre licence, which covers musicals, operas, plays, revues and dance shows.

If performing in a new venue it is necessary to submit the relevant application form, seating and stage plans and a fee. An inspection should then take place to ensure the venue meets the required safety standards in terms of:

*   Exits
*   Gangways and passages
*   Toilet facilities
*   Doors and direction of openings
*   Emergency lighting provision
*   Seating and layout of the stage

Animals

The Performing Animals Act (1925) requires that a person wishing to exhibit or train a performing animal should be registered. Local authorities may issue certificates having inspected the premises and conditions the animal is kept under. If you are considering using domestic animals, then write with proposals to the Environmental Service Department.

Children

The Children and Young Person Act (1963) under section 37 requires every child under 16 must be licensed unless he performs less than four days in a six month period. The number of hours and performances may vary depending on the age of the child, and what they are required to do. It is therefore advisable to contact the local education authority, which will advise on all conditions and issue the relevant licence.

Firearms

When using firearms in a production it is necessary to ascertain whether a licence is required. Under section 12 of the Firearms Act 1968 (as ammended by section 23 of the Firearms Act of 1988) special allowances were made for the use of firearms in a theatrical situation.

Firearms requiring a Part 1 Firearms certificate:

*   Real firearms including those adapted for firing blanks.
*   Purpose built starting pistols.

Firearms not requiring a firearms certificate:

• Firearms which have been deactivated, and stamped by a proof house.
• Replica or imitation guns.

A few suggestions for safe practice in the use of firearms:

• Guns and weapons must be kept locked up at all times.
• Never leave a gun or weapon unattended.
• The stage manager (or responsible person) will unlock the weapon and hand it to the relevant performer. Once used onstage the stage manager will collect it immediately, check and clean it if necessary then lock it up again.
• Ensure the performer has been trained in its safe use. Care should be taken as to its handling as pressure can escape from the top of the barrel and cause burns.
• No gun should ever be pointed directly at another performer or the audience. Aiming slightly upstage will be safer and will look just as convincing from the auditorium.
• All blank ammunition must be locked away in a strong box and limited to the correct number required for the run.
• All types of weapons should be covered if carried in public.
• The police must be notified if a weapon is lost or stolen.

The above information is by no means exhaustive and serves only to highlight the need to be attentive to the law. If in any doubt contact your local police firearms licensing department and an accredited supplier of weapons.

Health and safety training

In recent years several organisations have been formed offering courses in many areas of technical training, including Health and Safety:

1. Theatre Technical Training Services (TTTS)
2. Scottish Theatres Technical Training Trust (S4T)

Both trusts organise training in all aspects of the technical side of theatre for professionals, and S4T has recently recruited a Health and Safety Training Advisor to develop an advisory, information and training service for all S4T members.

3. Association of British Theatre Technicians (ABTT)

This organisation provides the exchange of information and establishment of best theatre practice between people involved in the technical aspects of live performance. It offers training, publications on codes of practise, conferences, seminars, trade shows, 'ABTT Update' (a quarterly magazine) and a website.

4. Independent Theatre Council (ITC)

Organises training in all aspects of theatre including management and technical courses in mainly small-scale theatre.

5. St John's Ambulance Service and The Red Cross.

It is extremely useful to have attended a First Aid course with one of the above organisations. There should be at least one first aider on duty during a performance, to deal with any medical emergencies that may occur.

Advice on any matters regarding Health and Safety can be provided by the national industry group for the entertainment industry 'The Health and Safety Executive', based in Glasgow. They publish a range of guidelines and advisory sheets.

CHAPTER 10

THEATRE UNIONS

'Oh come on, someone must want to be an equity dep?'

There are four unions offering membership to professionals in the theatre industry:

*   Equity (British Actors' Equity Association)
*   BECTU (Broadcasting, Entertainment, Cinematograph and Theatre Union).
*   Musicians Union.
*   Writers Guild

British Actors' Equity Association

British Actors' Equity Association, normally abbreviated to just 'Equity', represents actors, stage managers, singers, dancers, choreographers, variety, club and circus performers, theatre designers and directors and many others in the entertainment industries. Equity is an independent, non-party political, non-sectarian trade union. Equity membership can be obtained through engagements in the following areas of work:

Theatre:
> As a performer or stage manager in all forms of theatre, if you have undertaken paid work.

Directors, Designers and Choreographers:
> As a director, designer or choreographer if you have undertaken paid work.

Television, Films, Commercials and Radio:
> As a performer engaged on the appropriate contract.
> As a presenter on television or radio.
> As a walk-on, supporting artist or background artist, if you can show evidence of at least six days' work over a period of 12 consecutive months, undertaken on an Equity agreement (TV production only).

Singers:
> As a concert, session or pop singer if you can send evidence of one professional engagement.

Variety and Circus:
> As an artist who usually undertakes short term engagements or gigs you need to send contractual evidence of four of these within the last 12 months plus one forthcoming engagement.
> As an artist working on a long term engagement such as on a cruise ship, in a theme park, a circus or a holiday centre etc.
> As a dancer engaged in a cabaret floorshow or a dance troupe either in the UK or overseas.

Other Categories:
> As a student on a full time performing arts course of more than one year in length, you can take out student membership at a greatly reduced fee. If you are a student on an accredited dance or drama course, or studying in a music *conservatoire* or in theatre design, then you will be eligible for membership of Equity on graduation. If you are aged between 14 and 16 years of age and working for at least half the relevant adult rate you can become an Equity Youth Member.

If you have worked overseas:
> If you have worked professionally overseas and can provide proof of your employment, together with details of membership, if any, of the relevant union in the country or countries concerned, you are eligible for membership of Equity.
> This applies to UK and EU citizens, or those from other countries who have a work permit to work in the UK as artists.

Representation and bargaining rights

Equity's principal function is to secure the best possible terms and conditions for its members through collective bargaining and to make representations to Government and other bodies on matters of policy relating to the performing arts, film production and broadcasting.

Standard contracts laying down minimum terms and conditions have been negotiated with individual employers, or employers' associations, in virtually every area of entertainment: theatre, television, films, radio and recording, light entertainment and club work.

Contractual advice

Free advice in any case of dispute or disagreement in connection with professional engagements is available to all members in benefit via any office of the union. Legal protection is offered to members where necessary subject to the approval of the Equity Council.

Tax, National Insurance and state benefits

Members can obtain advice on tax, National Insurance and all employment-related state benefits. In appropriate cases the staff will prepare cases and represent members at appeals and tribunals.

Distribution of residuals and royalties

Equity is responsible for distributing royalty payments that it has negotiated for members in respect of repeats and reruns of television programmes and video and audio sales. In addition, in order to benefit from current and future European directives, Equity has established its own collecting society called BECS (British Equity Collecting Society).

Accident Benefit, Backstage Insurance and Public Liability Insurance

Equity provides free insurance to its members against accidents wherever they occur, together with free limited cover against loss or damage to possessions at work. In addition a group Public and Products Liability insurance policy covers Equity members for claims of up to £5 million at no cost. Further details are available from any Equity office.

Equity Regulations

It is necessary for the stage management graduate and new professional to understand the basics of the Equity regulations. It may be your first job in a small scale touring company, with responsibility for ensuring the performers' hours are kept within the Equity minimum working week. It is also reassuring to know what hours you are expected to work, and what breaks to observe.

There are four types of Equity agreement, (West End, Provincial, Subsidised Repertory and ITC) so do check which contract you are on, and get to know that particular agreement. I have formulated a very basic crib sheet, which highlights the hours and breaks observed on a Subsidised Repertory Agreement. This is how a typical working week might look without incurring overtime.

Crib sheet for Sub. Rep. Agreement (1999):

Periods of work   8.30am – 1pm
                   1pm – 6pm
                   6pm – 12am

Weekly hours   43 hrs

Meal breaks   1 hr between periods of work.
                   1³/₄ hrs between rehearsal and performance.
                   45 mins. Between curtain down and curtain up.
                   1¹/₂ hrs between performance and rehearsal.
                   15 mins. Coffee break in any 3 hrs.

Hours of work   Minimum 4 hr call (except a performance call)
                   12¹/₂ hrs in any one day (incl. Meal breaks).
                   11 hrs between end of evening call and the next day.
                   Minimum of 2 periods of work off each week.

Example of a typical 43-hour week:

Monday	AM 10-1 PM 2-5.15 Eve 7-10.30	 Performance	3 hours 3 hrs 15 mins 3 hrs 30 mins	9 hrs 45 mins
Tuesday	AM Off PM 2-5.15 Eve 7-10.30	 Performance	- 3 hrs 15 mins 3 hrs 30 mins	6 hrs 45 mins
Wednesday	AM Off PM Off Eve 7-10.30	 Performance	- - 3 hrs 30 mins	3 hrs 30 mins
Thursday	AM 10-2 PM Off Eve 7-10.30	 Performance	4 hours - 3 hrs 30 mins	7 hrs 30 mins
Friday	AM Off PM 1-5.15 Eve 7-10.30	 Performance	- 4 hrs 15 mins 3 hrs 30 mins	7 hrs 45 mins
Saturday	AM Off PM 2-6.15 Eve 7-10.30	 Performance	- 4 hrs 15 mins 3 hrs 30 mins	7 hrs 45 mins

Total Hours: 43

BECTU

BECTU is recognised locally and nationally as the union for all grades of staff working in film, TV and theatre, excluding performers and stage management.

BECTU negotiates pay rates and conditions for all its members. It also provides a range of services customised for its members from free public liability insurance to legal advice and assistance.

Musicians Union

The Musicians Union is the largest union representing theatre musicians in Europe. It negotiates all terms and conditions for its members annually with the Theatrical Management Association (TMA).

It offers a range of services such as legal and contractual advice, free public liability insurance, etc.

Writers Guild

The Writers Guild of Great Britain represents the interests of writers in film, radio, publishing, theatre and television.

Affiliated to the TUC, this trade union's function is to negotiate minimum terms for its members, and offers individual advice on contracts, etc.

General

Equity, BECTU, The Writers Guild and the Musicians Union are all core members of the Federation of Entertainment Unions and together with the NUJ provide greater lobbying power on behalf of theatre practitioners.

Some companies may offer a buy-out contract, or an in-house agreement, regardless of which union one is a member of. Do read these types of contracts carefully to ensure a 'fair deal'.

CHAPTER 11

THE JOB MARKET

'Unless you're a table top dancer, wig technician, self-contained solo artist
or an experienced stage door keeper it's another bad week...'

Finding a job

Once armed with the relevant qualification or apprenticeship experience, the next task is that of seeking employment in the theatre profession! As with any job these days, the choices are finite. There are only so many theatres in this country, employing one or two assistant stage managers.

Do not limit yourself to one particular area. It is important to be willing to move anywhere there is work, thereby expanding your choices. Here are a few pointers as to where to begin looking:

The Stage and Television Today   This weekly paper has a section for situations vacant, and most theatres and companies will advertise here first. Be realistic about the level of position you apply for and look at assistant's positions. There is no point in applying for a deputy stage manager's post if you are a graduate looking for your first job (unless it is for a small scale company, and even then the employers may require a couple of years relevant experience). It is wise for a student to begin buying this paper a year before they graduate to get a feel for the market and the natural ebb and flow of positions available. Do not give up too quickly, as even successful stage managers sometimes took a few months to land their first job.

Contacts and word of mouth   Keep a close ear to the ground in your own area to begin with, and whereever possible try to get part time work as a casual or usher at a local theatre. It can be beneficial to see as many shows as possible, and try to meet the stage management teams of that theatre, to get your face known, and to show an interest.

Head hunting   A very grandiose title and usually used in big business but applicable to the theatre business none the less. You will find that once you have found your first few jobs, and prove yourself to be reliable and successful, it is likely that word will get round, and if lucky you will be phoned up and offered further employment.

Placements   I cannot stress to the undergraduate enough how important your choice of placement is. Many graduates get their first job from the theatre or company they spent their placement with, myself included. When choosing your placement consider the ideal type of theatre or company you would wish to work for, then approach the relevant production manager. An employer is far more likely to offer an interview to someone who knows the company, fitted in well with the rest of the team, and has proved himself or herself to be reliable and capable of the job being offered.

The Stage Management Association (SMA)   A graduate of an accredited course, or anyone working in a professional stage management capacity, is eligible to join the SMA. Membership offers the following advantages:

Help finding work   Every month the SMA publishes a list of all members looking for work which is sent to over 600 potential employers of stage management.

Networking with other stage managers   Meetings are held four times a year in London during which members can raise any questions or concerns relating to stage management either in person or in writing. These meetings are usually combined with an event of interest to stage management (tour of a theatre, talk, demonstration etc)

CUELINE   Members receive a newsletter published eight times a year containing articles of interest, members' correspondence and a noticeboard.

Representation for Stage Management   The SMA is the only body representing professional stage management in the UK. It voices concerns to other organisations (Equity, Theatre's Advisory Council, TMA, ABTT) including Metier, who are working on nationally recognised Stage Management NVQ's as well as to the public and press.

Publications There are several useful publications available through the SMA, such as 'Notes for Company Managers', 'Notes for Stage Managers', 'Digs Lists' and 'Stage Management: A Career Guide'.

CVs and cover letters

Once you have scoured the *Stage* and decided which positions you wish to apply for, compile a suitably professional CV and cover letter. It may be the case that you have to phone or write for an application form, which should be diligently filled in.

Both cover letter and CV should be kept short and to the point. A production manager may receive between 25-50 applications for the one post, and does not have the time or inclination to wade through pages of information. It is important to make any paperwork neat, presentable and accessible to the reader using a word processor. Having your CV on disk means it can easily be updated or tailored to suit the job you are applying for.

Cover letters

The cover letter should contain the minimum of information stating where and when you saw the advert, and why you are applying. Do find out about the company, its artistic policies, the type of productions it stages and any other useful information which shows you have a specific interest in working for that company. It may also be useful to explain what specials skills you could bring to that particular stage management team, but keep it brief and formal. Let your personality shine through.

Curriculum Vitae

A typical CV might look like this *(see opposite page)*

Interviews

Once you have got an interview, take time to prepare for it. Find out more about the company, if you haven't already, including who may be on the interview panel and which shows you might be working on. If at all possible (and where relevant) visit the theatre beforehand, even see a show which will help put you at ease in a new environment. If you have to travel a fair distance, arrive in plenty of time to allow for a cup of coffee in the foyer. Get a feel for the theatre and browse the season's brochures.

- Prepare your attitude. Be convinced you want the job, and you are the person they are looking for.
- Be prepared to be positive about your own achievements and capabilities, finding a balance between blowing your own trumpet and outright boasting.
- Be willing to express enthusiasm, especially if you are last in and the panel may be flagging. Project yourself as someone who derives pleasure from life and work and is truly interested in that particular organisation.

Dougal Mackenzie

17 Treetops
The Glen
Watermead
KT123 4TS
Tel 01234 123456

DoB: 8/10/78

Equity member

Clean driving licence

Education:

1991-1996	Drumlanrig High School Hawick, Scotland	7 Standard Grades 3 Highers

Training:

1996-1999	Queen Margaret University College, Edinburgh	BA Stage Management/ Theatre Production

Professional Experience:

July-Sept 1997	Smirnoff Theatre Co., Edinburgh Fringe	ASM / LX operator
July-Sept 1998	The Grouse House, Edinburgh Fringe Venue	Crew / sound op.

Other:

June-Aug 1996	Scottish Youth Theatre, Glasgow	ASM / Crew
Dec 98 -	McLearys bar, Edinburgh	Part-time barstaff

References:

Mr Adams
Venue Organiser
The Grouse House
Edinburgh
Tel 0131 789 45678

Ms Alloa
Smirnoff Theatre Co.
Black Lane
Glasgow
Tel 0141 999 23456

- Keep smiling and maintain eye contact wherever possible. Keep fidgeting to a minimum.
- At assistant level you will not be required to wear a suit, unless it is ballet or opera, but you will need to be smart and tidy.
- Be prepared to answer the usual standard questions:

The five worst questions:

    'Tell me about yourself'
    'What is your major weakness?'
    'What will you be doing in five years time?'
    'How would your friends describe you?'
    'What has been your biggest failure?'

The five most asked questions:

    'Why do you want the job?'
    'Why should we give it to you?'
    'What interests you in our organisation?'
    'How have you benefited from your time at University?'
    'What have you learned from your work experience?'

- Have a few questions prepared to ask the panel. You may even write them down as no one will judge you if you produce a prompt card.

- If you haven't understood the question then just ask for it to be repeated. There is no right and wrong answer, so be confident in your responses. The panel are trying to get a feel for you as a person, and how you might fit in with the rest of the team; they are not marking a quiz card.
- If you are an undergraduate make use of the Careers Advisory Service who may be willing to set up mock interviews on request.

On my visits round theatres in the past few years, I have asked many different production managers what they are looking for in an ASM. These are a few of their replies:

'Hold a clean driving licence'.
'Good communicator and articulate'.
'Positive attitude'.
'Ability to maintain enthusiasm and sense of humour'.
'Really wanting to be an ASM'.

Too many graduates and young professionals have aspirations beyond their abilities and see the gradual growth of experience and building of a sound knowledge base as time consuming and unnecessary. Climbing the ladder too quickly can be detrimental to both the profession and the individual.

Never underestimate the benefits of networking. Keeping an eye on the 'Production News' and 'Situations Vacant' in *The Stage* can be useful in keeping up with new productions, and who has moved where. It is also important to keep your contacts book up to date.

Transferable Skills *by Paul Rummer (Bristol Old Vic Theatre School)*

It seems quite clear that training in theatre stage management equips people with widely applicable and transferable skills. At the heart of it lies the emphasis on project management, people skills, crisis management, logical thinking, good organisation of facts, data and schedules, working to deadlines, sheer hard work and above all applied common sense. The most important skill, which comes largely through experience, is being able to take the wider picture.

This ability to steer everyone along the same course with good humour and tact is exactly what is in short demand in so many walks of life and it is no surprise to find ex-stage managers turning up in a huge range of different jobs.

As the old TV and radio companies have been forced to fragment, the creation of an increasingly competitive freelance employment market has emerged. The increase in small production companies has mirrored the way freelance theatre employment has been for many years. Despite universities being awash with media courses there is still a skills shortage of trained practical people who can settle into jobs without further re-training. This can work to the obvious advantage of trained stage managers used to assimilating new jobs quickly (often a rep stage manager meets the company at the readthrough and three and a half weeks later the show is on!) Nevertheless, it is now possible to find work as a runner and move rapidly through to 1st assistant director or location manager in the same time as a theatre stage manager might move from ASM to production manager.

Finally it is worth considering the ease with which well-trained stage management students are able to transfer rapidly into other branches of the industry considered unavailable a decade ago. Theatre stage management find themselves equally at home in trade shows and conferencing as showcallers (equivalent to DSM), rigging, setting up staging and AV equipment (equivalent to technical ASM) or managing the overall organisation (equivalent to production management). They can find work on cruise ships (Disney now float one of the most sophisticated and automated shows in the world), or again themed events (currently the largest performance project in Britain is probably the Millenium Dome which is staffed largely by theatre people).

Likewise this horizontal transfer of skills is equally valid in TV, film or radio. The trick here is to understand the different names given to ASM, stage manager etc. Working the 'panel' in radio drama would otherwise be known as operating the mixing desk in theatres. Likewise '3rd assistant director' in TV is ASM. The skills are comparable but the different industries don't necessarily understand that fact. Thus success at moving horizontally into different areas is largely dependent on your ability to speak that industry's language.

'Can I run a flat by myself? Well, at the moment I still live with my mother.'

CHAPTER 12

INFORMATION AND COMMUNICATION TECHNOLOGY IN STAGE MANAGEMENT

Those seasoned travellers out there will remember the days when stage managers viewed the typewriter with distrust! Fortunately we are now catching up with the rest of the world (plus LX and sound departments, stage management budgets permitting). The younger professionals will take much of the new technology for granted but it is worth noting how far technological developments have come in just a short space of time, and how much they have enabled our working practices.

Computers

- Word processor: letters, templates, memos and general paperwork.
- Database: information storage and retrieval, such as a props and furniture storage information system, contacts, credits, master borrow book.
- Spreadsheets: budget control.
- Desk top publishing: leaflets, posters, newspaper headings etc.
- Drawing packages: setting plots and relational diagrams etc.
- Route-finders for touring.
- Voice activation for dyslexics or the visually impaired.

Image scanners

- To reproduce images from books, scan the image and print out. Very useful for period labels, packaging, newspapers etc. A colour copier will perform a similar function, but does not allow the storage of the original image as one can with the scanner when saved to disk.

Internet

- The World Wide Web: a vast resource of images and information that is now invaluable in terms of props and furniture research (so much quicker than plodding down to the local library).
- E-mail: Allows quick and efficient communication throughout the world. Internal e-mail is already replacing the manual system of daily distribution of paperwork to production

departments in some companies. It is especially useful for larger companies whose production departments may be situated in different locations or on tour.

Mobile phones, fax, pagers

• Touring companies in particular have come to rely heavily on these forms of communication. Faxing plans is useful, but can also now be done using e-mail.

Digital camera

• A wonderful replacement for the old Polaroid. Once the image is taken, it can be stored on disk, reproduced on screen or printed out. Allows the director and designer to view images of props and furniture, and once stored can be used to build up a furniture catalogue or used as the basis for setting plots. The image can then be sent anywhere in the world, such as other theatres wishing to borrow certain items, via e-mail.

Computer Aided Design (CAD)

• A 3-D visual design package, which can generate a 'virtual' model of a set. Any element of the model can be manipulated (lighting, colour, scenic pieces etc). This allows directors, designers and production managers to test the successful or indeed unsuccessful scenic movement.

Programmable cueing systems

• As shows become increasingly complicated, some larger companies are turning to programmable cueing systems to enable the DSM to cue what would otherwise be impossible sequences.
• There are a few systems in development, and one developed in conjunction with The Oxford Sound Company and installed at *The Royal Exchange* in Manchester which is PC compatible. The only British system currently available on the market is called Softcue.

Softcue is a memory cue light system, which brings the technology of lighting and sound systems to the theatre's prompt corner. Whilst the system can be used in conventional mode using 'Standby' and 'Go' switches, Softcue has the unique advantage of being a memory system with total recording, playback and fault reporting facilities.

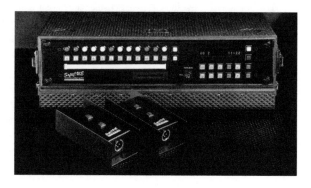

Shows can be recorded via simple key sequences that allow full recording, playback and review for up to 48 cue light outstations and up to six shows. It is now installed on many West End musicals and world-wide venues.

Computerised prompt desks

The use of such packages is the subject for much heated and controversial discussion among professionals. The strongest objection is on the grounds of Health and Safety, eg: the ability for the DSM to maintain overall control of a cueing sequence in the case of any deviations from the original show. All systems do provide override methods, but adequate training is essential.

Many computerised show control systems have been used in multi-media trade shows and conferences for years. The main difference here is the lack of performers and therefore the lower risk factor.

There are a few fully integrated computerised prompt desks available internationally such as the 'Stage Manager 1200HD'. This package developed and produced by Richmond Sound Design in Canada includes the computer, monitor, MIDI interface and software as a total solution for centralised control of all technical production elements including lighting, sound, machinery, video, projection, process control, pyro and virtually any other system capable of MIDI control.

The Millenium Dome has developed its own customised digital cuelight system, inhibited by the show caller. This show control system uses digital communications protocol, with a midi control component.

Northern Light, Edinburgh have developed a Stage Management Desk using touch screen programmable control panels for cue, effects and access to multi zone paging, calls and video facilities. There are separate screen images for cue lights, ancillary systems, switching and video images from any remote camera. All screen images can be accessed quickly through one screen or, on the larger desk, two screens – with one screen designed for cue lights and all other switching and video pictures on the second.

The future

After training stage management students for a number of years, and recalling the fear of operating my first book on the opening night, I realised there was a real need for a facility to enable the student DSM on the book to practise cueing outside a live performance. In 1997 I undertook research to investigate the development of a program which would fulfil this need.

Peter Byard (of Peter Byard Associates) carried out the majority of the technological research and programming investigation. Together we developed a software package proposal based on a PC with outboard cuelights. The software package could consist of 3 modules:

Training module

The screen would show a theatrical stage production reacting in real time to DSM operation (via the cuelights). For example, on starting up the programme, the screen/monitor shows a pros arch, tabs in, tab warmers and house lights up. On depressing the correct cuelights (i.e. Fly Q 1 & LXQ1) the tabs go out, houselights and tab warmers fade, then on the next set of cues (LX2 & CL1), which could either be on screen or an outboard set of cuelight switches, the lights come up, actors enter and the play begins. Much like a computer game the program would encourage the student to use the same artistic and interpretative skills in controlling the show as they would operating the real thing. Developing a feel for the creativity and dynamics of the theatrical moment is the most important skill a DSM learns whilst cueing a show. The program would respond to the events cued, so the students would get instant feedback to their cueing actions.

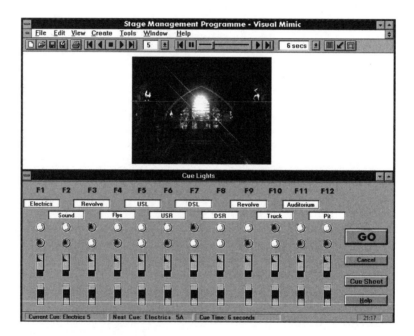

Rehearsal and show operation mode

Imagine the DSM in rehearsals using a laptop, instead of the hand-written prompt copy. An imported script and blocking, use of props and cueing sequences being added in as appropriate. Once into a production week, if set to show running mode and integrated with a computerised cueing system it could be used to operate and trigger cues for the show (using MIDI interface).

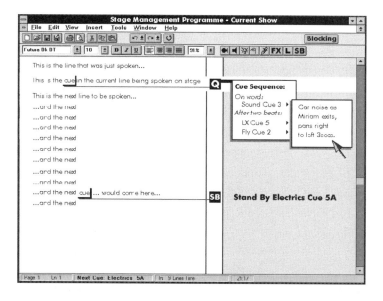

Mimic mode

If one used 2D representations for the set and moving pieces of scenery, imported from the designer's story board perhaps, one could create a simplified version of 3D vector graphics (using bit map graphics) mentioned earlier under CAD. This would provide the significant benefit of simpler and far easier data entry, and could perform the same function of allowing the designer and director to see 2D representation of scenic movement during the rehearsal process. If then linked to the word processor in rehearsal mode the cueing sequences could then be pre-programmed before the technical rehearsal.

Our research showed that all the above was possible and now all that remains is to find funding to develop the programme and market this new use of today's technology. It may be years before the profession can see the benefits of the 'rehearsal and show operation' programmes but I'm sure that any stage management student and young professional would agree that the training package is needed now!

CHAPTER 13

FURTHER READING

The following are a few of the books I have found useful over the years.

Antique reference guides

- Millers Antiques Guide   MJM Publications & Newnes
  (Professional handbook)   ISBN 0-905879-43-0

- Victorian Household Album   Collins and Brown
  by Elizabeth Drury and Philippa Lewis   ISBN 1-85585 221-7

- Food and Drink (19c sources)   Dover Publications
  Selected by Jim Harter   ISBN 0-486-23816-4

- Chairs Through the Ages   Dover Publications
  Edited by Harold H. Hart   ISBN 0-486-24348-6

- Packaging Source Book   McDonald Orbis
  by Robert Opie   ISBN 0-35617665-7

- The Art of the Label   Quarto publishing Ltd
  by Robert Opie   ISBN 0-671-65441-1

When researching a period show always start in your local library.

Stage Management

- Stage Management, A Gentle Art   A & C Black
  by Daniel Bond   ISBN 0-7136-4551-2

- The Staging Handbook   A & C Black
  by Francis Reid   ISBN 0-7136-4176-2

- Stage Management and Theatre Administaration   Phaidon
  by Menear & Hawkins   ISBN 0-7148-2516-6

- Score Reading   Cambridge Educational
  by R. Bennett   ISBN 0-52126949-0

Lighting, Sound, and Props making

- The Stage Lighting Handbook   Pitman, London
  by Francis Reid   ISBN 0-7136-2957-6

- Sound and Recording   Focal Press, Oxford
  by F. Rumney & T. McCormick   ISBN 0-2405-1487-4

- Create Your Own Stage Props   A&C Black
  by J. Glovier   ISBN 0-7136-2419-1

- The Theater Props Handbook   Betterway Publications
  by J. Thurston   ISBN 0-9326-2088-4

Management

- Essential Manager's Manual   Dorling Kindersley
  by Robert Heller and Tim Hindle   ISBN 0-7513-0400-x

- Managing Stress   Gower Publishing Ltd
  by Christine C. Brewer   ISBN 0-566-07946-1

- Assert Yourself   Gower Publishing Ltd
  by Cal Lemon   ISBN 0-566-07945-3

- Essential Delegation Skills   Gower Publishing Ltd
  by Cala L. Brown   ISBN 0-566-67944-5

- The Tao of Leadership   Gower Publishing Ltd
  by John Heider   ISBN 0-566-07472-9

Theatre, Film and Television References

- Contacts   Spotlight
                                                   ISSN 1366-4646

Health and Safety

- Fringe Safe   The Festival Fringe Society
  by Julian Sleath and the Festival Fringe Society   ISBN 0-9525059-2-4

- The HMSO 6 pack   'Management of Health and Safety at Work'
                    'Manual Handling'
                    'Personal Protective Equipment'
                    'Workplace Health, Safety and Welfare'
                    'Work Equipment and Display Screen Equipment'
                    'COSSH'

- 'Guide to Fire Precautions in Existing Places of Entertainment'. (Also from HMSO)

- 'Production Safety and Risk Assessment' by Eastbrooks Safety Services.

CHAPTER 14

TEMPLATES

Show Report

Show:			No:
Signed:			Date:

Act / Interval	Up	Down	Time

Total running time:

Total playing time:

Notes:

Comments:

Cc:

Production Risk Assessment

Production: Date:

Production Manager:

Hazard	Potential loss	Risk factor before	Precautions	Risk factor after

1-7 Low priority (acceptable risk)	8-14 Priority (requires attention)	15-25 High priority (unacceptable risk)

Calculating the Risk Factor

Severity	x	*Likelihood*
5 – Death / multiple casualties		**5** – Inevitable
4 – Severe injuries		**4** – Likely
3 – Serious injuries / time lost in excess 3 days		**3** – Quite possible
2 – First Aid required / no time lost		**2** – Unlikely
1 – No visible effects		**1** – Improbable except in freak circumstances

Rehearsal Call

Show: **Date:**

Time	Company	Call	Location

CC:

REHEARSAL NOTES

Show:	No:
Date:	Signed:

SM/Props

Set

LX

Sound

Wardrobe

CC:

Props List

Page	Item	Source	Reh	Act	Des	Dir	Pass

Petty Cash

Show: **Department:**

Date	No.	Description	Amount
	1		
	2		
	3		
	4		
	5		
	6		
	7		
	8		
	9		
	10		
	11		
	12		
	13		
	14		
	15		
	16		
	17		
	18		
	19		
	20		
	21		
	22		
	23		
		Total:	

Cue Synopsis

Show: **Date:**

Page	Cue	Description	Input Point	Time up/down	Notes

Credits List

Show: **Date:**
Credit deadline:

Credit name	Contact name	Items	Department

Budget Analysis Sheet

Show:
Dept:

Date:
Budget:

Date	No	Item	Who	Initials	PC/OF/T	Cost	Balance

Borrow Form

Date:

On loan to:

On loan from:

Items	Condition	Value

Date for return:

Signature of recipient:

Actual return date:

Confirmation of return (print name):

CHAPTER 15

GLOSSARY

Actual – A prop used in performance.

Ad lib – Words or lines in a performance not true to the script.

Administrator – The person who controls overall spending within the company, and oversees all administration staff.

Agent – A representative who negotiates contracts and fees for performers.

Amateur – Persons engaged in theatrical performance without payment.

Aside – Lines spoken in a play to be heard by the audience and not other characters.

ASM – Assistant stage manager.

Audience – Spectators at a performance.

Auditions – An interview for a role in a performance.

Auditorium – The area of the theatre in which the audience is situated.

Backstage – The area of the stage and theatre which is not public.

Bar bells – Bells sounded FoH to alert the audience to the start of the performance.

BECTU – Broadcasting, Entertainment, Cinematography and Theatre Union.

Beginners – The call given backstage five minutes before curtain up.

Blackout – Darkening or absence of light onstage.

Blacks – Black clothing worn by the backstage team during the show.

Blocking – Notation of performers' moves in the prompt copy.

Blues – Blue backstage working light.

Book – Otherwise known as the 'prompt copy'. A record of all the performers' moves, calls and cues as they relate to the script.

Borrow – An item borrowed for use in a performance.

Borrow book – A book containing a complete record of all borrowed items for a particular show.

Box – Otherwise known as the control room, where lighting, sound, and sometimes the DSM cueing the show are situated.

Break – The end of a period of work, or pertaining to a meal break.

CAD – Computer aided design.

Call – Notification of work periods given to the company i.e. rehearsal call. A backstage or FoH announcement.

Cans – Headsets used as part of the intercom system.

Carpenters – Persons who build the set.

Cast – The performers in a show.

Casual – Backstage crew employed on a show by show basis.

Centre line – A hypothetical reference line running up and down the centre of the stage.

Checks – Pre-show verification that all items are ready, and all equipment working.

Chippie – A carpenter.

Choreographer – The ballet, dance or movement designer or arranger.

Clearance – Short for 'front of house clearance', which is notification from the front of house manager that the audience is settled in their seats and the show may begin.

Cloth – A painted or dyed piece of material hung backstage as part of the set.

Comestibles – An item which is used or consumed nightly, and supplied new for each performance.

Comp – Abbreviation of complimentary, or free, ticket.

Company – Collective term for the performers and often stage management.

Corner – Short for the prompt corner where the DSM cues the show, usually down stage left.

Corpse – Unintentional laughter by a performer during a show.

COSHH – Control of substances hazardous to health.

Costume – Clothing worn by the performer specific to their character.

Costume call – Also known as costume parade when each performer 'parades' their costume in front of the director(s), and designers.

Credits – Written recognition given in the programme to those who have assisted with items for a production.

Crew – Casual or full time staff employed to work backstage on a particular show.

Cross – A performer's movement from one part of the stage to another.

Cross fade – The fading up of one cue while fading down another.

Cue – (1) A word or action by one performer to signal a response from the next. (2) A verbal or visual signal usually given by the DSM to confirm the timing of an action for the operators or performers during a show (a lighting or sound fade, an entrance, an offstage effect etc).

Cuelights – A set of lights (red for stand by, green for go) which are situated around the backstage areas and control room to cue operators, stage management and performers.

Cue synopsis – A session during which all cues are discussed in detail and their timing and positions written in the prompt copy.

Curtain – The drapes hung at the furthest point downstage to mask the audiences view of the stage.

Curtain call – The original intent of the 'bow' at the end of a performance was to give the performers the opportunity to thank the audience for attending their production!

Cut(s) – Words, lines, props, furniture, cues etc. no longer included in the show.

Cyc – Abbreviation for cyclorama which is a large, often curved cloth hung upstage to donate sky, or vista affording creative lighting opportunities.

Dark – A 'dark' theatre is one which has closed for a period of time, often to allow for maintenance work to be carried out.

Dead – A marked point for the positioning of scenery, and in flying terminology donating the 'in' or 'out' position.

De-rig – To take down electrical equipment or flown pieces from the grid.

Designer – The person responsible for the overall visual look of a production.

Desk – Lighting, sound or prompt desk refers to the operating console for that particular discipline.

Digs – Accommodation for the members of a theatrical company.

Director – The person responsible for the cohesion of all elements of a production from the design to the performer's characters and moves.

Doorslam – A piece of apparatus specifically built to reproduce the sound effect of a door opening or closing.

Downstage - The area of the stage below centre.

Drapes – Any soft material used in the set or masking.

Dress – Short for dress rehearsal. A full run-through onstage without stops integrating all elements of the set, effects, costumes, props, furniture etc.

Dressing – Elements of the set, props or furniture which are used to give the piece authenticity but not actually handled or referred to by the performers.

Dry tech – A run-through onstage incorporating all technical elements without performers.

DSM – Deputy stage manager.

Edibles – Any props which are eaten during the show.

Electrics – Referring to the team in the lighting and/or sound department.

Entrance – A performer entering the stage area to engage in a scene.

Equity – The union representing performers, stage management, designers, directors etc.

Event – A numerical reference to a particular cue or sequence of cues.

Exit – A performer leaving the stage area.

Extras – Performers employed to fill a scene, usually without specific lines, or characters.

Fade – To increase or decrease a light or sound level.

Finale – The spectacular scene at the end of a performance.

Fire proofing – Spaying or soaking materials with fire retardant liquid.

First night – The official opening night of a show, often with invited audience and press.

Fit up – Building the set onstage.

Fittings – Performers called to wardrobe to try on costumes requiring alterations.

Flat – A flat wooden framed piece of scenery clad in canvas or ply.

Fly – To raise or lower a piece of scenery via the flying system.

Fly floor – The platform from which the flyman operates the flying system.

Flyman – The person employed to rig and fly scenery.

Focusing – To adjust the size and position of the light beam of rigged lamps as required.

FoH – Front of House, the audience reception area, which may include the box office, bar and restaurant.

FTF - Fibrous T- frame for removing debris from the stage area.

Full House – The auditorium at full capacity.

Gaffa – Short for gaffa tape, strong 2" wide tape essential for all theatre work.

Get in – To move the set, costumes, props, furniture and equipment from vans, workshops or storage areas into the stage area.

Get out – To remove all elements from the stage to vans, workshops, or storage areas.

Go – The command to activate or respond to a cue. If visual the cuelight will show green.

Green room – The backstage rest and refreshment area for the company.

Grid – A metal or wooden 'grid' from which pulleys of the flying system or fixed lines are attached for flown equipment.

Ground plan – A scaled drawing of an overhead view if the stage and/or set.

Heads – Abbreviation for 'heads up'. A warning shouted onstage to alert occupants of falling debris/equipment from above.

HoD – Head of department.

Houselights – The lighting in the auditorium.

Line – (1) A request for a prompt. (2) A line of a speech. (3) A length of fibre or wire rope.

LX – Abbreviation for lighting.

LX tape – Slang for insulating tape which is available in assorted colours ideal for marking up.

Mark – A piece of tape donating a setting position.

Mark up – (1) A representation of the set, using tape and sometimes elements of the set in a rehearsal room. (2) The action of marking up the rehearsal room floor with tape to represent the set.

Masking – A piece of scenery (usually a flat or soft drape) concealing the onstage technical areas from the audience's view.

Monitor – (1) A screen backstage reproducing the onstage view via a camera FoH, allowing stage management and the company to have a clear view of the action onstage. (2) A backstage speaker reproducing the onstage sound.

Notation – Written representation of the performers moves.

Notes – A session after the technical, dress or first few performances where the director and production manager will iron out problems with the backstage team and performers.

Opposite Prompt – Stage right or opposite the prompt corner.

Page – (1) The action of opening a door or drawing back soft masking to allow the performers a smoother entrance or exit. (2) To call a performer to the stage.

Paintshop – The area or workshop in which the sets are painted.

Passed – A piece of furniture or prop which has been accepted by the director and designer.

Personals – Small props set in the dressing room at the top of the show.

Photo call – A session where specific shots of the play are set up, for publicity.

Plotting session – A session during which all the lighting and sound cues are decided by the director and designers, and are then recorded in a memory board or manually.

PM – Production manager.

Practical – A prop or piece of electrical equipment which has to work.

Pre-show – The period of time before the show goes up.

Preview – The first performance open to the public, usually at a reduced price, giving the company the opportunity of trying out a new piece before the opening night.

Prompt – A request by a performer for the prompter to give them a line if they have dried.

Prompt copy – Otherwise known as 'the book'. A record of all the performers moves, calls and cues as they relate to the script.

Prop – Smaller items onstage used by the performers.

Props call – A session before the technical during which the stage manager checks through all the props and furniture with the designer and director.

Quick change – A fast costume change backstage, usually involving the assistance of a dresser(s).

Read through – A seated company reading through the play together for the first time.

Rehearsal – A practise of scenes or sections of the performance culminating in the technical and dress rehearsals.

Rehearsal call – The period of work the performer is called to rehearse.

Rehearsal prop – A prop that is a rehearsal substitute for the actual.

Repertoire – A stock of pieces the company have prepared to be played in rotation.

Repertory – A theatre company engaged for a season to produce a series of plays.

Re-set – To set back all elements of the set, furniture and props in preparation for the next performance.

Returns – The activity referring to returning all borrowed and hired props, furniture, costumes and equipment at the end of a show.

Review – A critique of the production by an outside party appearing in the press.

Rig – To hang and position all electrical and flown sound equipment.

Role - A character part given to a performer.

Revolve – A large circular or rectangular truck on wheels with a central pivot point, which can be sunken into the stage floor or set on top and turned around to different positions revealing different settings.

Rostra – A raised platform of any shape or size.

Runners – Strips of carpet or matting laid backstage to prevent noise of footfall and to help guide the company along safe routes.

Running plot – A list of cues and/or activities to be performed by the backstage team or operators.

Safety curtain – A large non-flammable barrier separating the stage and auditorium, situated just behind the proscenium arch. In the event of a fire this is lowered to prevent the spread of fire.

Scale – A ratio of size used in representing measurements in working drawings, ground and lighting plans.

Scene – A section of a play.

Scenery – The elements which make up the set.

Scene breakdown – Can be referred to as an availability chart; it shows which characters are in which scene at a glance.

Scene change – The resetting of set, props or furniture to change the location or time in a play.

Setting line – The line, usually downstage, to which all other points of the design are set to.

Setting plot – A list, with relevant diagrams, showing the positions of elements of the set and all props, furniture, costume and dressing at the top of the show.

Setting up / back – To re-set all elements of the set, props, furniture and costumes.

Show report – A written report of the show giving details of running times, deviations from the script, audience size, and any operation problems that may have occurred.

Sight line – A line drawn on a ground plan showing the view from the audiences eye to what can be seen onstage.

SM - Stage manager.

SMA – Stage management Association.

SMgt – Stage management.

SQ – Sound cue.

Stand by – The instruction given to alert operators, backstage team and performers that a cue is imminent. If visual, the cuelight will show red.

Strike – (1) To disassemble the set, lighting and sound rig and remove props, furniture and costumes from the stage area. (2) To remove any item from the stage during the show.

Tabs – The drapes just behind the proscenium, masking the stage from the audience.

Tab warmers – The illumination on the tabs before the start of the show.

Technical rehearsal – The session(s) during which all elements of the show are put together onstage for the first time and the production is run from beginning to end with stops to iron out any problems.

Truck – A piece of scenery on large castors.

Understudy – A person employed to 'study under' a lead performer's role in case the lead is absent.

Upstage – The area of the stage above centre.

Ushers – Persons employed to show the audience to their seats, sell programmes, collect tickets.

Visual – Usually refers to a cue which an operator takes themselves, rather than being cued by the DSM, to ensure spot-on timing (such as switching on a light switch).

Walk – To 'walk the lights' is to move about the stage slowly, facing out to enable the lighting designer to check the desired effect of a lighting state during the plotting session.

Wardrobe – (1) The department responsible for making and supplying the costumes.
(2) The storage area for costumes.

Wings – Offstage areas to the left and right of the acting area.

Working drawings – Scale drawings of the scenery used by the carpenters to build the set.

Working light – Lighting used during onstage work independent of the lighting rig.

INDEX